DECORATIVE TECHNIQUES
FOR WOODTURNERS

DECORATIVE TECHNIQUES
FOR WOODTURNERS

HILARY BOWEN

GUILD OF MASTER CRAFTSMAN PUBLICATIONS

First published 1996 by Guild of Master Craftsman
Publications Ltd, 166 High Street, Lewes,
East Sussex BN7 1XU

ISBN 1 86108 015 8

Designed by Christopher Halls at Mind's Eye Design
Set in Goudy
Printed and bound in Great Britain by the University Press,
Cambridge

Metric/imperial conversions
Although care has been taken to ensure that imperial
measurements are true and accurate, they are only conversions
from metric. Instances will be found where fractionally
differing metric measurements have the same imperial
equivalents. This is because, in each particular case, the *closest*
imperial equivalent has been given, usually to within $\frac{1}{32}$ in
either way.

CONTENTS

ACKNOWLEDGEMENTS

I would like to thank:
Bob Carabine for his patience and encouragement.
Robert Lee for his invaluable assistance with Chapter 10.
And all those people (particularly members of Hampshire Woodturners Association)
who have given me information and tips along the way.

INTRODUCTION

There has been a surge of interest in woodturning in many countries over the last few years. This interest has been accompanied by a growth in experimentation, and the development of techniques which can be used to decorate woodturned items.

One of the first questions which springs to mind is, 'Why decorate woodturning at all?' Many people argue that wood has a natural beauty of its own, and that by applying additional decoration we are in some way detracting from this. To an extent, I would agree with this viewpoint. Certainly, many of the most stunning pieces of woodturning are those which have no additional decoration at all: beautifully turned burrs and natural-edged bowls, for example, where the colour, the grain pattern and the natural shapes and lustre of the wood have no need of further enhancement. Indeed, to add further embellishment would not only be unnecessary, but would spoil the natural beauty of the material.

In addition, the skill of the turner can produce exquisite forms from plain timbers: the superb lines and curves produced need no further decoration. Consequently, it is important always to consider whether any decoration is needed at all, and the answer may well be no.

Having said that, decoration can mean something as simple as the addition of a single line of beading at the rim or foot of a vessel. This is a commonly used method of adding interest and emphasis to a particular area. Decoration does not have to be complex and time consuming, nor indeed, innovative. It can refer to simple, long-established techniques perfected by turners over the centuries.

There are so many different methods of decorating wood that it would be impossible to cover all of them in the scope of one book. I have therefore been selective and have chosen those techniques which are, by and large, fairly straightforward and which do not require high levels of skill. Most turners who have a basic level of turning competence should have no difficulty with any of the methods described here.

A basic level of skill and knowledge of common turning techniques is assumed: that is to say, there are no explanations of *how to turn* the items in this book. Rather, it is aimed at those people who already know how to turn basic items such as bowls and boxes, and who are familiar with appropriate methods of chucking, finishing and so forth.

The purpose of this book is to promote ideas and to give examples of a wide range of methods which can be adapted to suit the individual. Above all else, I hope that it will help to emphasize the importance of experimentation.

Thought needs to be given to the appropriateness of any particular decorative technique – some techniques may enhance one object, yet spoil another. The nature of the item concerned, the timber, the shape and the form all need to be considered carefully when deciding how a piece may best be enhanced.

A measure of restraint is also required. Do not be tempted to use too many different forms of decoration on one piece – one or two is generally enough. It is important not to overdo it and spoil the effect. Very often, it is not what is put in that counts, but what is left out.

The projects described throughout the book are given as examples only, and you should feel free to alter the details and adapt the techniques to suit your own purposes. It is certainly not intended that the examples given should be copied slavishly to the last detail.

Likewise, the methods of chucking which are illustrated here are not mandatory – feel free to use whichever chucking methods suit you. I would, however, recommend the use of those methods which allow the workpiece to be returned to the lathe after completion. In some instances, this is essential; in others, it is merely convenient. I tend to favour the expanding dovetail collet as a chucking method, since I find it reliable and am able to return work to the lathe at a later date with no problems of centring. Consequently, I frequently cut decorative dovetail recesses in the bottom of my work. Of course, this method of chucking is not always possible or appropriate, so you should consider chucking techniques carefully before embarking upon any project.

Most of the decorative techniques described here begin either after the item has been turned, or part-way through the turning process. For each project, the starting point is described, and it is from that point that the instructions begin. No instructions are given regarding the turning which leads up to that starting point.

Each project serves to exemplify a particular technique – usually in the simplest way possible. It is hoped that readers will choose to take some of these techniques further – to adapt and refine them, and to develop them further to create more complex forms if they so wish.

Similarly, the precise methods which have been described are those which I have found easy and manageable, but you may use slightly different methods to achieve the same results. Flexibility is all-important.

I have tried, where possible, to include a wide range of objects for the turning projects, and to use a variety of timbers. I have also tried to include a varied selection of decorative techniques which are versatile and which may appeal to a wide range of tastes and interests.

Aspects of health and safety are dealt with at the appropriate points, and a general guide to health and safety in the workshop is provided in the Appendix (see page 164).

If this book promotes interest and provides inspiration, it will have achieved its aim.

PART ONE
USING METAL

Metal Rod and Tubing

Inlaying Wire

Molten Metal

Laminating with Sheet Metal

INTRODUCTION

Metal can be used in a variety of ways to decorate woodturned items. The techniques employed are fairly straightforward, and although some require a little patience, the extra effort is worthwhile because the effects can be quite dramatic and can enhance an otherwise ordinary object.

SELECTION OF TIMBER

The visual effect is best when there is a contrast between the colour of the wood and that of the metal. Since most metals tend to be rather pale in colour, it is wise to select dark-coloured timbers. Similarly, it is best to choose timbers which have an even colour throughout, with no pronounced grain pattern. Examples of suitable timbers are ebony, blackwood, padauk, purpleheart and some of the darker rosewoods, although many other timbers will also be suitable.

SELECTION OF METALS

There are various suitable metals available, although your choice may be limited to those which are readily accessible to you. Choose fairly soft metals where possible – brass is probably the hardest I would use, since harder metals are more difficult to work. Pewter, silver, copper, aluminium and brass are all suitable for inlay and laminating work. For casting purposes, special low melting-point alloys are required.

AVAILABILITY OF METALS

Most good craft and hobby shops stock metal in various forms: sheets in a range of thicknesses, rods and tubes of different lengths and diameters, and wire in various forms. Suppliers of non-ferrous metals are an alternative source. It is sometimes difficult to acquire silver wire from normal retailers, but many mail-order companies supply it in a range of thicknesses. Some will even supply it in square cross-section. Jewellers (especially those who carry out repairs on the premises) may sell silver wire in small quantities, and may even be prepared to 'draw' it down to whatever thickness you require. Pewter blocks and other low melting-point allows can be obtained fairly easily through mail order.

There are, of course, cheaper sources – scrap metal merchants, junk stalls at jumble and car boot sales, the contents of attics, garages and rubbish skips, and so on. All these can reveal scraps of metal sheeting, wire, rods and tubing, so it is always worth keeping a lookout.

FINISHING

In order to obtain a high lustre on the metal you will need to use successively finer grades of sandpaper, finishing up with 1,000 grit if possible: the finer the abrasive, the better the lustre. If a very fine-grained, very dark timber such as ebony or blackwood has been used, the metal can be polished using metal polish with the lathe running. This will give it a really high shine and will not harm the surrounding wood. It is unwise to use metal polish on coarse-grained, paler timbers, however, since the black residue will discolour the wood.

SAFETY

Avoid breathing in fine metallic dust by wearing a dust mask, *at the very least*. When turning, always wear a face shield as protection against stray flying scraps of metal. (These are the same precautions that you should take when turning wood anyway.) Some of the low melting-point alloys contain elements of cadmium and lead, so take care when handling these and always wash your hands thoroughly afterwards.

1

METAL ROD AND TUBING

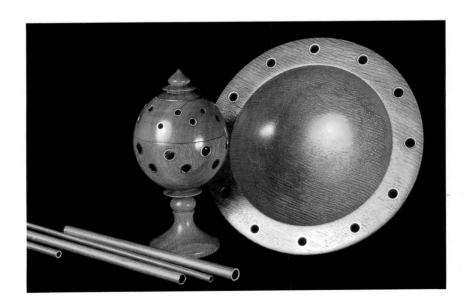

◆ Availability and selection ◆ Basic technique ◆

PROJECTS

◆ Brass tubing in a bowl rim ◆ Brass rod in a goblet base ◆

ESSENTIAL EQUIPMENT

Drill bits to match tubing and rod diameters
Mini-hacksaw
Cyanoacrylate glue (superglue)
Basic turning tools and materials

RECOMMENDED EQUIPMENT

Indexing ring

AVAILABILITY AND SELECTION

Metal rod and tubing is most commonly available in brass, aluminium and copper, in a wide range of diameters and lengths (see Fig 1.1). The diameter

FIG 1.1
Metal rod and tubing is available in a range of diameters.

required will depend on both the size of the item to be decorated and the general design of the decoration. In some instances, different diameters can be incorporated very effectively in one item.

The choice of metal will depend to an extent on the timber to be used. Colour is one aspect: as we have already noted, the best effects are usually obtained where there is a contrast between the colour of the metal and that of the wood. Copper, for example, would probably be a poor choice to use with reddish-coloured woods, while a silver-coloured metal such as aluminium would look particularly good with very dark timbers.

Another consideration is the density of the timber in relation to the hardness of the metal. If a less dense, soft timber is to be used, it is wise to choose a soft metal, such as copper or aluminium. Harder metals, like brass, are better suited to harder timbers, because during the sanding process a soft timber tends to be worn away more readily than a hard metal, creating a ridge of metal instead of a flat surface. (There are ways of avoiding this, however, so it should not be regarded as a hard and fast rule.)

BASIC TECHNIQUE

The basic technique of inlaying rod and tubing consists of embedding the metal in the wood, by inserting and gluing it into a pre-drilled hole in the selected position. The size of the drill bit must correspond to the diameter of the rod or tubing; if you are unsure of the correct size, it is worth drilling a pilot hole into a piece of scrap wood to check first. The rod or tubing should fit snugly into the pre-drilled holes and can be secured in place with superglue.

When drilling holes to receive the metal, it is imperative that the drill bits are absolutely sharp. It is a good idea to keep a spare set of new drill bits especially for this type of work and to ensure that they do not become blunted by other DIY jobs where the precision of cut is less important. Using blunt drill bits can result in irregular-shaped holes and grain tear-out on the undersides of surfaces.

There are two methods of cutting and fitting the metal; either short lengths can be pre-cut to the required depth before insertion and gluing, or one end of the rod or tube can be inserted into the hole, glued in place, and sawn off just above the surface of the wood when the glue is dry. Either method will work well, and I would recommend that you use whichever seems easiest and most appropriate. Both methods are illustrated in this chapter. Whichever is used, it is important to ensure that the embedded lengths of metal protrude only *fractionally* above the surface of the wood after insertion, so that sanding can be kept to a minimum.

BRASS TUBING IN A BOWL RIM

The starting point for this project is a bowl 50mm (2in) high, with a maximum diameter of 147mm ($5\frac{3}{4}$in) and a rim width of 19mm ($\frac{3}{4}$in). Native Australian pear was the wood used here (see Fig 1.2). In this example, a dovetail recess was cut in the base during turning, for use with an expanding dovetail collet. Consequently, it could be remounted on the lathe easily for the following procedure.

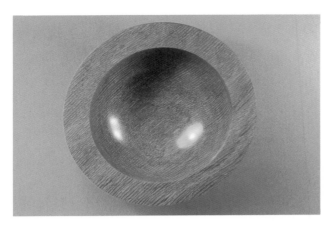

FIG 1.2
Starting point: an Australian pearwood bowl.

FIG 1.3
Use a skew chisel to true-up the bowl rim.

MATERIALS AND METHOD

Brass tubing 7mm ($\frac{1}{4}$in) diameter

1   With the bowl mounted securely in the chuck, switch on the lathe and true-up the surface of the rim using a sharp skew chisel (see Fig 1.3).

2   The next step is to mark on the rim the position of the holes in which the tubing is to be embedded. One method of doing this is to attach an indexing ring (see Fig 1.4) to the lathe behind the chuck. (Indexing rings can be home-made, as illustrated, or can be purchased from suppliers of turning accessories.) The headstock can thus be secured at regular intervals by means of a locating pin through the holes (see Fig 1.5).

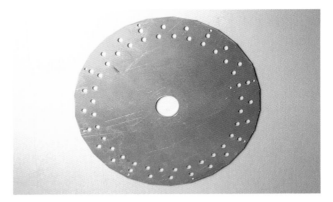

FIG 1.4
An indexing ring, home-made from a flat metal disc drilled with rings of holes at precise points. In this example, the outer ring is divided into 24 equal segments, the holes being equidistant and 15° apart, and the inner ring into 32 segments.

FIG 1.5
The headstock is secured in position by a locating pin.

3   Drill a hole through a cylinder of spare wood, and secure the cylinder vertically in the tool rest. Insert a pen horizontally through the hole and make an ink mark on the bowl rim (see Fig 1.6). (You may use alternative methods of

FIG 1.6
Mark the positions for the holes on the bowl rim using a pen pushed through the holes in the scrap-wood cylinder.

locating the indexing ring and securing the pen. The somewhat makeshift system shown is only one of a number which may be used.)

4   When the first mark has been made, remove the locating pin from the indexing ring, turn the ring the required distance and replace the locating pin in the next appropriate hole. Make another mark with the pen, and then repeat the process until all the marks have been made. In this example, 12 equidistant holes were required, so the outside ring of holes was used, with the locating pin inserted into alternate holes. In this fashion, the workpiece is gradually rotated through 360° at 30° intervals until all the points have been marked on the bowl rim (see Fig 1.7).

FIG 1.7
All 12 hole positions have now been marked around the bowl rim.

TIP

It is not essential to use an indexing ring. Any other method of marking out equidistant points on a circle is quite acceptable. An alternative method for subdividing and marking a bowl rim, using transparent plastic, is illustrated in Chapter 2 (see page 23).

---

5   Using an appropriate size of drill bit – in this example 7mm ($\frac{1}{4}$in) – carefully drill the holes right through the rim. There are a number of ways of doing this. One is to drill with the workpiece still in position on the lathe, using a hand drill. Alternatively, the workpiece may be removed and the holes drilled using a drill press. Fig 1.8 shows the holes drilled around the edge of the bowl rim.

FIG 1.8
Drill the 12 holes at the marked positions.

6   Measure the depth of the bowl rim: in this example, 3mm ($\frac{1}{8}$in). Select a length of brass tubing 7mm ($\frac{1}{4}$in) in diameter and saw off 12 pieces, each approximately 1mm ($\frac{1}{32}$in) longer than the depth of the rim.

7   Insert the small pieces of brass tubing into the holes in the bowl rim, ensuring that the edges of the tubing are slightly proud of the surface of the rim on both the upper and lower sides. Glue in position using thin superglue – the glue can be trickled in gently once the tubing is in position (see Fig 1.9).

FIG 1.9
Glue the tubing in position in the 12 holes.

TIP

Before applying superglue to the surface of any piece of wood, always coat the surrounding area first with the type of finish you intend to use, e.g. sanding sealer. Failure to do so will result in the wood being stained by the glue.

8   When the glue has dried thoroughly, gently cut back the rough edges of the tubing which protrude above the rim flush with the surface, using a skew chisel, bowl gouge or any other appropriate tool you prefer.

TIP

It is quite acceptable to use ordinary woodturning tools to cut metal which has been inlaid into wood, as only a very small surface area of metal comes into contact with the blade in comparison to that of the wood. The blade will not be harmed, although it will become blunt more quickly than when used on wood alone. The rate at which this happens will depend on the hardness of the metal and the amount to be cut through: soft metals, such as pewter and silver, will not blunt the blade significantly more than certain hard timbers. When cutting metal embedded in wood in this way, just be prepared to sharpen your tools rather more frequently than normal.

9   With the lathe turning, sand the upper and lower surfaces of the bowl rim, starting with 180 grit sandpaper and working through the grades, finishing with 400 grit.

10   Apply any required finish. In this example, sanding sealer and carnauba wax were used.

11   Finally, clean up the insides of the brass tubing. In all probability bits of dirt, dust and even glue will have collected there. Scrape away any hardened glue, and then polish the metal using ordinary metal polish applied with a scrap of cotton wool or cloth wrapped around the end of a matchstick. The edges of the tubing flush with the bowl rim can also be polished with metal polish provided the timber is

dark-coloured and dense. In this example it would not be advisable, as the timber is too light in colour and too coarse grained. If a high lustre is nevertheless desired, it can be achieved using an extremely fine abrasive, such as 1,000 grit. Fig 1.10 shows the finished bowl. Fig 1.11 shows a pomander in purpleheart in which brass tubing of different diameters has been embedded using the above technique.

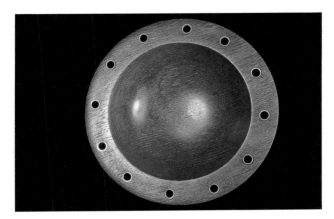

FIG 1.10
The finished pearwood bowl.

FIG 1.11
A purpleheart pomander decorated with brass tubing in a range of diameters.

BRASS ROD IN A GOBLET BASE

The starting point for this project is an ash goblet 138mm (5$\frac{7}{16}$in) high, with a rim diameter of 67mm (2$\frac{5}{8}$in) and base diameter of 72mm (2$\frac{7}{8}$in) (see Fig 1.12). Because ash is rather pale in colour, it is not ideally suited to being inlaid with metal. To enhance the visual effect, I therefore decided to embed the metal rod in a ring of black resin. It is obviously not essential to do this, and would be unnecessary with a darker-coloured wood. Nevertheless, it is interesting to see how two separate techniques may be combined to good effect. Chapter 12 deals specifically with the use of resins.

MATERIALS AND METHOD

Brass rod 3mm ($\frac{1}{8}$in) diameter

Black resin

1   This particular goblet is one which I had turned some time previously, so in order to remount it on the lathe it was inserted into a jam-chuck (see Fig 1.13). The tailstock was then brought up for support at the 'cup' end with a scrap-wood bung.

2   Using a parting tool, cut a recess in the base of the goblet (see Fig 1.14). The recess should be 2mm ($\frac{1}{16}$in) deep, 6mm ($\frac{1}{4}$in) wide and 6mm ($\frac{1}{4}$in) in from the edge of the base (see Fig 1.15). Remove the goblet from the lathe and place it in an upright position.

FIG 1.13
Remount the goblet on the lathe in a jam-chuck.

FIG 1.12
Starting point: a simple ash goblet.

FIG 1.14
Cut a recess in the goblet base, ready for filling with resin.

3 Mix up the black resin and pour it into the recess so that it settles *slightly* above the surface of the goblet base. It is possible to do this without the resin running over the sides because it is a thick liquid. The base of this goblet is fairly flat (see Fig 1.12) and the resin therefore settles in it easily. Clearly, this procedure would not have been possible with a more steeply sloping base. (For full details on mixing and using resins, see Chapter 12.)

4 When the resin is *completely* dry, mark a series of points around the ring of resin to represent the positions where the brass rod is to be embedded. The number of marked points will depend on the diameter of the base, the diameter of the rod to be used, and personal taste, not to mention level of patience! In this example, 3mm ($\frac{1}{8}$in) rod was to be used and 16 points were marked (see Fig 1.16). In order to mark the points at equal intervals, and indexing ring may be used, as described in the previous project.

5 Using a 3.2mm ($\frac{1}{8}$in) drill bit, drill a hole at each marked point to a depth of approximately 2mm ($\frac{1}{16}$in).

6 *Either* pre-cut the rod into 3mm ($\frac{1}{8}$in) lengths and glue each length in position using thin superglue (as described in the previous project), *or* insert the end of the whole length of rod into one hole and again glue in position. When the glue has dried, saw off the remaining length of rod flush with the surface of the goblet base using a mini-hacksaw (see Fig 1.17). Repeat this procedure for the remaining holes until they have all been inlaid with brass rod (see Fig 1.18).

7 Remount the goblet on the lathe and, with the lathe running, gently sand the base until smooth. Use successively finer grades of sandpaper, finishing with 1,000 grit.

8 Apply sanding sealer or melamine to the wood on the base in the usual way, then cut back using wire wool and buff with a soft cloth.

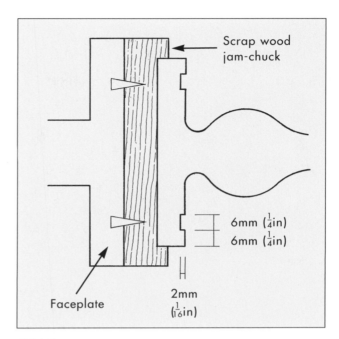

FIG 1.15
Cut a recess in the base of the goblet, using a parting tool.

FIG 1.16
When the resin has dried completely, mark 16 equidistant hole positions around the ring.

FIG 1.17
Saw off the glued rod flush with the surface of the goblet base.

FIG 1.18
Glue brass rod in position in all 16 holes.

9   Polish the resin and brass inlay using ordinary metal polish, applied with a piece of cotton wool or cloth wrapped around a matchstick. This is best done with the lathe running. If using a pale-coloured timber, such as the ash in this example, make sure that no metal polish spills over on to the surrounding wood, as this will discolour it. Buff with a soft cloth and apply a wax finish to the entire goblet.

Fig 1.19 shows the finished goblet.

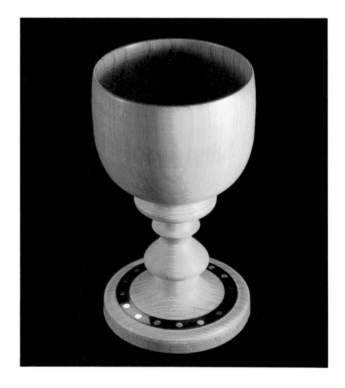

FIG 1.19
The finished goblet, with brass rod inlaid in resin.

2

INLAYING WIRE

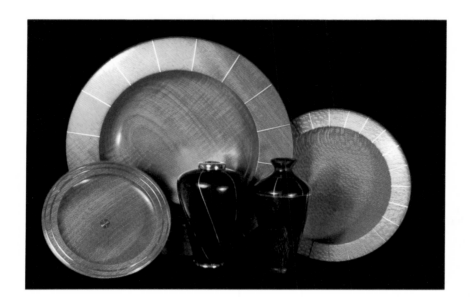

◆ Selection of wire ◆ Selection of timber ◆ Planning ◆ Basic technique ◆

PROJECTS

◆ Brass wire inlaid around a bowl rim ◆ Brass wire inlaid transversely across a bowl rim ◆
◆ Silver wire inlaid around a vase neck ◆ Diagonal inlays of silver wire ◆
◆ Silver wire inlaid along the grain of a lamp base ◆

ESSENTIAL EQUIPMENT

Mini-hacksaw
Craft knife
Superglue
Basic turning tools and materials

RECOMMENDED EQUIPMENT

Indexing ring
Miniature precision drill with glass-engraving
cutter attachment

The techniques used for inlaying wire in woodturned items are fairly straightforward and simply require a little patience. In the five projects in this chapter, a range of carefully selected timbers are inlaid with brass and silver wire in a variety of configurations, demonstrating just some of the unusual and striking effects that can be produced by experimenting with these techniques.

SELECTION OF WIRE

The most commonly available wires are silver, copper and brass, although you may well have access to other metals. As always, the contrast in colour between wood and metal is crucial in selection, although price may also be a factor. Silver wire is more expensive than copper or brass, but has the advantage of being slower to tarnish. Be careful that you do not buy silver-plated copper wire by mistake – the price should give you an indication.

The thickness of the wire is not critical, but it is best to aim for something between 0.8mm (0.0315in) and 1mm (0.0394in). Wire thicker than this can be used, but it is worth remembering that the thicker the wire, the less malleable it will be. Wire thinner than 0.8mm (0.0315in) is quite acceptable, but technique then becomes more important. This is because wire has a circular cross-section: in other words, it is as wide as it is deep, and width and depth are important considerations in the inlaying process, since the thinner the wire, the less of it will be embedded below the surface of the wood. This need not matter if you have carried out all the procedures very accurately, and if your workpiece is running absolutely true, but it does mean that there is no margin for error, and any uneven sanding (or over-sanding) will result in the wire being sanded away completely in one or more places. The thicker the wire, the greater your margin of error!

SELECTION OF TIMBER

The usual considerations regarding colour and density apply equally to selecting timber in which to inlay wire. Dense, fine-grained timbers, such as rosewood, blackwood and ebony, are particularly suitable, as metal polish can then be used during the finishing stage to polish up the wire to its maximum. With coarse-grained timbers, the black residue from the polish will become embedded in the grain, causing discoloration of the wood. Black woods, such as ebony, are best of all, since their dark colour is beautifully enhanced by the bright metal and they are not discoloured by the polish.

Choose timber without any pronounced figure, since variations in colour or highly decorative grain patterns are best left unadorned. Their natural beauty needs no further enhancing, and the pattern would detract from the visual effect of the wire. In this respect, timbers to be avoided might include zebrano, Brazilian tulipwood and so on.

Of course, these are not hard-and-fast rules, and exceptions to them can occasionally work well.

PLANNING

Having chosen the object you wish to inlay, the first decisions are aesthetic and concern the nature and design of the inlay. For example, you will need to decide which type (or types) and thickness of wire will be used, whether there will be one inlay or several and how the position of the inlays will be marked out. You will also need to determine whether the inlays will be in the same plane as the rotation or whether the grooves will need to be cut by hand (see page 15). It is a good idea at this stage to draw a sketch of the item, indicating where the various inlays are to be.

Next, you will need to decide at which stage during turning the inlaying will be done. In some instances it is appropriate to do this at the end, when the item is virtually finished and the turning more or less complete. Indeed, it is even possible to inlay an item long after it has been turned and removed from the lathe – a bowl which retains a recess in the base and can be remounted easily on the lathe is a good example.

It may be necessary to do the inlaying at some point midway through the turning, if the later stages would otherwise make the inlaying procedure difficult or impossible. Such decisions are all part of forward planning, and most woodturners are used to planning the stages of a project in advance, especially where more than one chucking method is used.

DIRECTION OF INLAY

During the planning stage, you will need to decide where exactly you wish the wire to be inlaid on your chosen item. Will it follow a particular pattern? Do you require a single ring of wire or a series of rings? Do you wish the lines of wire to be straight or curved? These decisions will largely be determined by the shape of the item: for example, a bowl might be decorated by bands of wire inlaid into the rim following the line of the circumference, while a vase might have rings of wire encircling it, perhaps at the shoulder, lip or base. In these examples, the direction of the inlay is in the same plane as the rotation of the wood when it is turning on the lathe, forming a complete ring or circle (see Fig 2.1). In other words, the groove into which the wire is to be

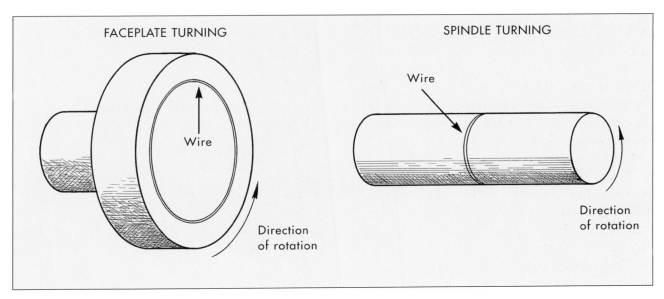

FIG 2.1
Wire inlaid in the same plane as the direction of rotation.

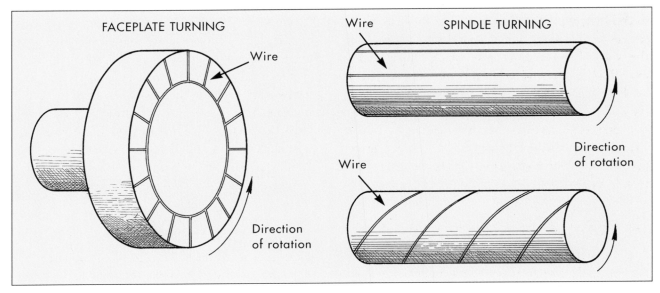

FIG 2.2
Wire inlaid in a different plane to the direction of rotation.

embedded can be made in the wood using a sharp tool while the lathe is turning. This is the quickest, easiest and most accurate method of cutting the groove.

Sometimes, however, you may wish to inlay the wire in such a way that it does not lie in the same plane as the rotation. This would be the case with lines of wire running the length of a vase, for example, or radiating out from its lip or from the rim of a bowl. In these cases the groove must be cut by hand, using a mini-hacksaw (see Fig 2.2).

BASIC TECHNIQUE

Although methods for cutting the groove may differ, the basic principles remain the same for any type of inlay. The basic procedure given below is for the easiest method, where the wire is inlaid in the same plane as the rotation and the groove can therefore be cut with the lathe running. This method is the same for both spindle and faceplate turning.

CUTTING THE GROOVE

1   Work out the position of your inlay and mount the workpiece on the lathe. With the lathe running, use any sharp-pointed tool (such as a small parting tool held sideways) to inscribe a small groove in the surface of the wood to mark the position of the inlay.

2   This small marker groove must now be widened and deepened until it is precisely the right size and shape to accept the wire. This stage is crucial. It is fairly straightforward to achieve the correct width, and this can be tested at intervals to see if the wire 'fits' the groove. However, the *shape* and *depth* of the groove are critical.

The groove should be *square* (not V-shaped), so that the wire lies in it correctly. This is an important step because, as Fig 2.3 shows, a V-shaped groove will not allow the wire to embed correctly: either it will be seated too high on the surface of the wood or, if the groove is deeper, the gaps at each side will be too wide. This cannot be achieved with a small parting tool alone. I have two home-made

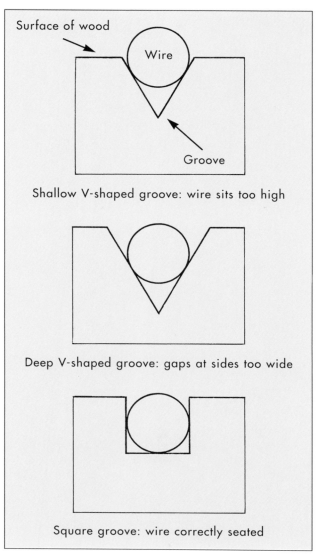

Shallow V-shaped groove: wire sits too high

Deep V-shaped groove: gaps at sides too wide

Square groove: wire correctly seated

FIG 2.3
The shape of the groove is very important.

tools, either of which is satisfactory for cutting a square. One is an old screwdriver, which has been ground at the end to create a cutting tool of exactly the right shape and width (see Fig 2.4). The other tool has been made by inserting a masonry nail into the end of a small handle and grinding the end into a flattish point (see Fig 2.5). Both of these tools work well, but any small tool can be used provided you are able to make a square groove with it.

Always remember, if you grind old tools to new shapes, they may need to be re-tempered afterwards.

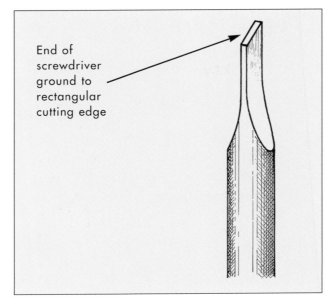

FIG 2.4

A screwdriver adapted for cutting a square groove.

End of
screwdriver
ground to
rectangular
cutting edge

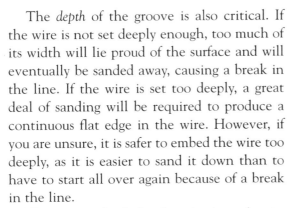

FIG 2.5

A tool for creating a square groove, made from a squared-off masonry nail inserted into a small handle.

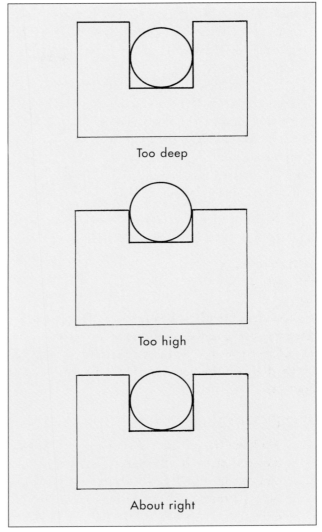

Too deep

Too high

About right

FIG 2.6

The depth to which the wire is embedded is critical.

The *depth* of the groove is also critical. If the wire is not set deeply enough, too much of its width will lie proud of the surface and will eventually be sanded away, causing a break in the line. If the wire is set too deeply, a great deal of sanding will be required to produce a continuous flat edge in the wire. However, if you are unsure, it is safer to embed the wire too deeply, as it is easier to sand it down than to have to start all over again because of a break in the line.

The correct depth for the wire is so that its top is approximately level with the surface of the surrounding wood (see Fig 2.6). At this depth, after minimum sanding the wire will be flattened evenly without removing too much of its depth or too much wood. The thicker the wire, the deeper the groove will need to be in order to accommodate it. The narrower the wire, the more critical the depth of the groove, because narrower wire is more readily sanded away.

It does not matter if the groove is *slightly* too wide. The malleable property of the metal enables it to spread very slightly during sanding to fill the gap. This is why, after sanding, the wire appears thicker than its original width.

3   When you feel that the groove is the right width, depth and shape, test it by placing a piece of the wire in it to see if the fit is snug.

EMBEDDING THE WIRE

1   Place one end of the wire in the groove, pushing it well down. Put a small drop of superglue on it to secure the end in place.

2   When the glue has set, stretch some more wire into the groove, pulling it down into the groove as far as it will go. (If only a short length of wire is to be inlaid, the remainder of its length can be embedded all in one go.) Trickle some more glue over the wire, allowing it to run into the groove. Repeat this procedure all the way round until you reach the place where you started (see Fig 2.7).

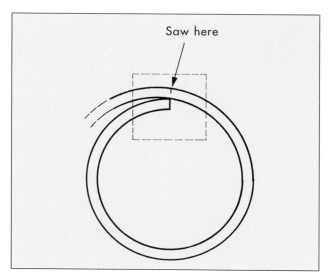

FIG 2.8
Saw part-way through the wire, using a sharp craft knife.

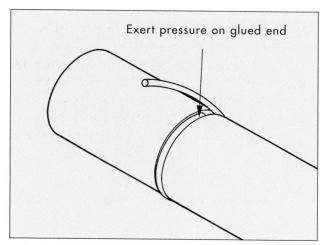

FIG 2.7
Continue to embed the wire in the groove until you reach the point at which you started.

3   When the glue has set, pull the free end of the wire round so that it rests on top of the glued end. With a sharp craft knife, saw a little way through the free end at the point precisely above the glued end (see Fig 2.8). Do not attempt to saw through the wire completely, or you risk damaging the surface of the wood. Gripping the wire firmly at its point of contact in the wood, move the free end up and down until it breaks off in the position of the saw cut (see Fig 2.9).

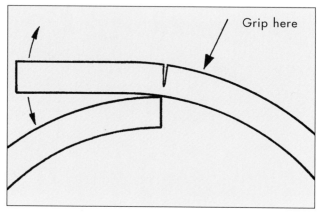

FIG 2.9
Move the free end up and down until it breaks.

4   If necessary, this rough end can be filed flat using a miniature metal file (see Fig 2.10). Embed the free end and glue it in position (see Fig 2.11). The join should be barely visible.

TIP

Do not use the superglue too liberally. An excess can be messy, and may result in the groove becoming filled with glue, which then sets before you have a chance to embed the wire. It is better to use just enough glue to secure the wire, and then, when the wire is seated, trickle a little more gently around the wire to ensure that it is secure.

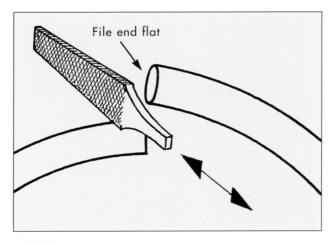

FIG 2.10
If necessary, file the rough end using a miniature metal file.

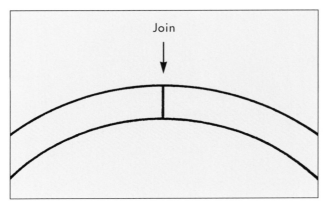

FIG 2.11
Glue the free end in position: the join should be barely visible.

SANDING AND FINISHING

1   At this stage the whole area around the embedded wire will look rather messy – do not worry! When the glue is completely dry, sand lightly with approximately 180 grit sandpaper. Continue to sand until the wire is flattened all along its length.

2   Move on to a finer grade of sandpaper, sanding gently. Continue to work through the grades, sanding gently, until you reach 400 grit or even finer. 1,000 grit wet-and-dry paper (used dry) can be used to finish off.

3   If you have used a very dark, close-grained wood, such as ebony or blackwood, you can polish the wire further using ordinary metal polish. If a coarse-grained and/or lighter-

coloured wood has been used, do not use metal polish as it will discolour the wood.

4   Apply any preferred spirit- or oil-based finish to the wood in the usual way.

CUTTING THE GROOVE BY HAND

As already mentioned, when the wire is to be inlaid in a direction other than the plane of rotation, the groove must be cut by hand with the lathe stationary. This takes longer, and particular care must be taken to ensure that the groove is exactly the same width and depth all along its length. This is not easy and requires a little practice, but it is very important because if the depth of the groove varies, the wire will be embedded at varying depths. Some areas of the wire will therefore require more sanding than others, and this is likely to result in some areas being over-sanded, causing the wire to break.

Use a mini-hacksaw to cut the groove, choosing one with a blade roughly the same width as the groove you need to cut. Some hacksaws have interchangeable blades, for cutting metal or wood. A metal-cutting blade is best, at least for making the initial cuts, because the finer teeth offer better control.

1   Mark out the position of the groove(s) using a pencil or pen.

2   Saw gently along the marked lines with light, even strokes. When the whole groove has been cut, check over its entire length to see if the depth is the same all the way along, and make any necessary adjustments.

3   Place a piece of the wire in the groove to check the fit. When satisfied, the procedures for embedding the wire are the same as previously described on page 18.

A FINAL CONSIDERATION

It is worth thinking about the hardness of the wire relative to that of the wood. Silver is a soft metal, copper medium and brass relatively hard. If you are inlaying a soft or medium wire into a hard or medium wood, there is no problem. Sometimes, however, you will wish to inlay a hard metal, such as brass, into a softer wood. The problem here is that during the sanding process, the wire will tend to be sanded away more slowly than the surrounding wood creating a ridge in which the wire will then sit (see Fig 2.12). This does not really matter, but the effect is much better if the wire is flat and the surface smooth.

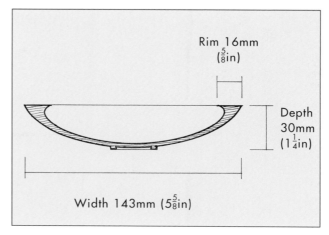

FIG 2.13
A section through the mahogany bowl.

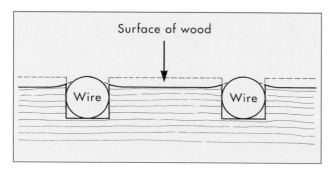

FIG 2.12
A ridge is sometimes formed with hard metal wire inlaid in a softer wood.

In order to overcome this, embed the wire slightly *below* the surface of the surrounding wood. Then, using a gouge or chisel, cut back the surface slightly so that effectively you are slicing off an extremely thin layer from the top of the wood and the wire all in one go, with a smooth finishing cut, to create a flat surface with the wire flattened along its length. A *very* light touch is required for this, in order to avoid cutting too deeply. After this, only the minimum of light sanding is required.

BRASS WIRE INLAID AROUND A BOWL RIM

The first project involves inlaying wire in the same plane as the rotation, creating a continuous ring and enabling the groove to be cut with the lathe turning.

The starting point for the project is a bowl of 30mm (1¼in) deep with a diameter of 143mm (5⅝in) and internally overhanging rim width of 16mm (⅝in) (see Fig 2.13). The mahogany bowl in Fig 2.14 has a central circular inlay of brass in the bottom, which was added as extra decoration at a previous stage and is not part of the procedure described below.

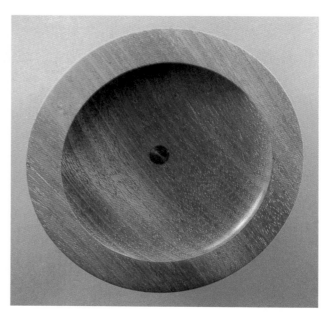

FIG 2.14
Starting point: a plain mahogany bowl.

MATERIALS AND METHOD

Brass wire, 1mm (0.0394in) thick

1 With the workpiece mounted on the lathe and the lathe running, inscribe a small marker groove in the flat surface of the rim, 4mm (⅛in) from the outer perimeter, using a parting tool or similar (see Fig 2.15).

2 Extend this groove using the appropriate tools until it is the precise width and depth required for the wire. Check to see that the wire fits snugly into the groove.

G 2.15
Inscribe a marker groove in the bowl rim using a parting tool or similar.

3 Repeat steps 1 and 2 to make a second groove 6mm ($\frac{1}{4}$in) from the first, towards the centre of the bowl (see Fig 2.16).

4 With the lathe stationary, embed one end of the wire in the first groove and secure it in place with a drop of superglue (see Fig 2.17). In this example, the bowl – still attached to the chuck – may be removed from the lathe and placed on a table. It is often easier to perform this stage with the rim of the bowl horizontal.

5 Continue to embed the wire, a few centimetres at a time, securing with glue as you go.

FIG 2.16
Make a second groove 6mm ($\frac{1}{4}$in) in from the first.

21

FIG 2.17
Start to embed the brass wire in the first groove, securing with superglue as you go.

FIG 2.19
Embed wire in the second groove in exactly the same way as for the first.

FIG 2.18
Glue the free end of the wire so that the join is barely visible.

FIG 2.20
The finished bowl, inlaid with concentric rings of brass wire.

6   Cut the free end of the wire to the correct length and glue securely into the groove. The two ends should abut exactly (see Fig 2.18).

7   Repeat steps 4–6 with the second groove (see Fig 2.19).

8   Starting with 180 grit sandpaper, sand the rim until the wire has been flattened along its length. Continue to sand with successively finer grades, finishing with 400 grit minimum. Apply the required finish.

The finished bowl is shown in Fig 2.20.

BRASS WIRE INLAID TRANSVERSELY ACROSS A BOWL RIM

In this project the wire is inlaid in a different plane to the rotation, so the grooves must be cut by hand. The starting point here is a ropalla bowl of similar design to that in the previous project, with a depth of 45mm ($1\frac{3}{4}$in), a width of 190mm ($7\frac{1}{2}$in) and an internally overhanging rim of 21mm ($\frac{7}{8}$in) (see Fig 2.21).

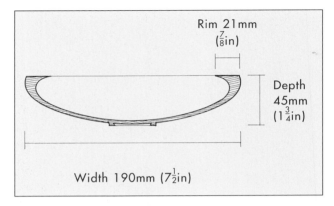

FIG 2.21
A section through the ropalla bowl.

MATERIALS AND METHOD

Brass wire, 1mm (0.0394in) thick

Transparent plastic for template (optional)

1   Mark out the lines for the grooves, which should be evenly spaced and positioned so that they appear to radiate from the centre of the bowl, across the rim. Either use an indexing ring (see Chapter 1), or make a template from transparent plastic, the thicker the better. The template can be kept and used again for a similar project at a later date.

2   With the aid of a protractor, draw a series of radial lines on to the plastic, as accurately as possible. Also draw on the position of the bowl rim. Place the template on a piece of scrap paper and, using a sharp point, pierce tiny holes at the points of intersection between the radials and the bowl rim lines (see Fig 2.22).

3   Place the template on top of the bowl rim, making sure that it is aligned carefully so that the bowl rim lines lie in exactly the right place. It is easier to do this if the bowl is removed from the lathe and placed horizontally on a flat surface, as shown. If the bowl has just been turned, it can be removed from the lathe while still attached to the chuck. Using a fine-point pen, mark small dots around the rim through the holes in the template (see Fig 2.23).

4   Using the same pen, join up each pair of dots so that the radials are clearly marked (see Fig 2.24).

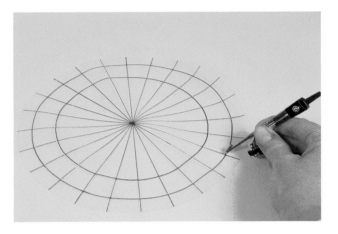

FIG 2.22
Pierce tiny holes at the intersections between the radials and the rim lines.

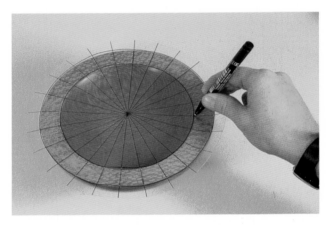

FIG 2.23
Mark dots through the holes in the template, using a fine-point pen.

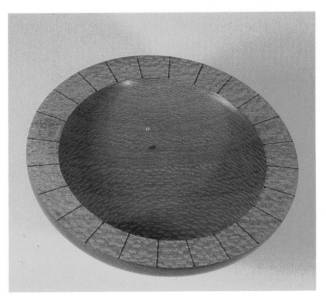

FIG 2.24
Join the dots to form radial lines.

FIG 2.25
Saw a groove along each marked line, using a mini-hacksaw.

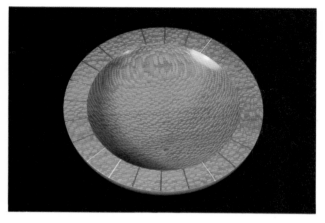

FIG 2.27
The finished ropalla bowl, with brass wire inlaid transversely across the rim.

FIG 2.26
Embed brass wire in the grooves.

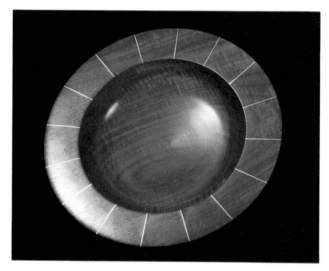

FIG 2.28
A larger bowl of similar design, this time in purpleheart with silver wire inlay.

5   Using a mini-hacksaw, carefully saw grooves along the marked lines (see Fig 2.25). Take care to saw to the correct width and depth, testing with the wire in the usual way.

6   Embed the wire and glue in place (see Fig 2.26).

7   Remount the bowl on the lathe. Sand as for the previous project and apply the required finish. The bowl is now complete.

Fig 2.27 shows the finished bowl. Fig 2.28 shows a larger bowl of similar design, using purpleheart and silver wire.

SILVER WIRE INLAID AROUND A VASE NECK

This project incorporates the two previous methods, inlaying wire in both the same and a different plane to the rotation. Both methods of cutting the groove are therefore involved. The starting point is a partially finished blackwood vase 140mm ($5\frac{1}{2}$in) high, with a shoulder width of 70mm ($2\frac{3}{4}$in) and a foot width of approximately 30mm ($1\frac{1}{4}$in) (see Fig 2.29).

FIG 2.29
Starting point: a part-finished blackwood vase.

MATERIALS AND METHOD

Silver wire, 0.8mm (0.0315in) thick

Transparent plastic for template (optional)

1   With the lathe running, inscribe a marker groove approximately 2mm ($\frac{1}{16}$in) below the widest part of the shoulder (see Fig 2.30).

2   Extend this groove until it is the correct width and depth for the wire, and check that the wire fits snugly into the groove (see Fig 2.31).

3   Embed one end of the wire in the groove and secure it with glue (see Fig 2.32).

4   Continue to embed the wire all the way round the groove. Cut the free end at the correct position and embed with glue, holding it in place until the glue has set (see Fig 2.33).

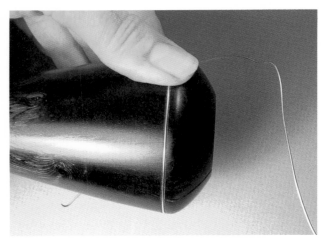

FIG 2.31
Check that the wire fits snugly into the groove.

FIG 2.32
Glue the end of the wire into the groove.

FIG 2.30
Inscribe a marker groove just below the widest part of the vase shoulder.

FIG 2.33
Hold the second end of the wire in place until the glue has set.

FIG 2.34
Mark six radial lines from the vase neck to the silver wire at the shoulder.

FIG 2.36
Complete the groove using a sharp craft knife.

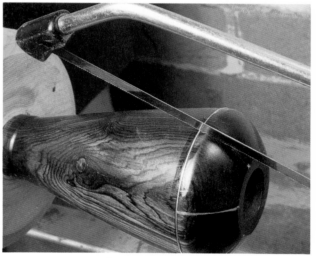

FIG 2.35
Gently saw a groove along each marked line, using a mini-hacksaw.

FIG 2.37
Embed silver wire in the radial grooves.

5   Mark six radial lines from the neck of the vase to the silver wire at the shoulder, using an indexing ring or template (see previous project), or even simply a pair of compasses (see Fig 2.34).

6   Using a mini-hacksaw, saw gently along the marked lines to make the grooves (see Fig 2.35).

7   When you get close to the silver wire which is already embedded, you will not be able to finish cutting the groove with the hacksaw or

you will saw through the wire. Use a sharp craft knife to complete the cutting (see Fig 2.36).

8   Embed the silver wire into the radial grooves in the usual way (see Fig 2.37) and sand.

9   Before applying the final finish, polish the vase with metal polish.

In this example, a violet rosewood neck and base were added to complete the vase. Fig 2.38 shows the finished piece.

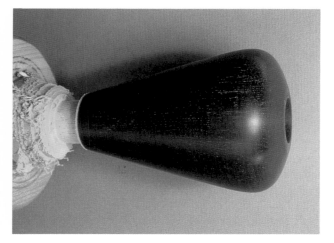

FIG 2.39
Starting point: a blackwood vase, still attached to the faceplate via a piece of scrap wood.

FIG 2.38
The finished vase, complete with silver wire inlay and violet rosewood neck and base.

FIG 2.40
Mark a series of six equidistant dots at the base, shoulder and foot of the vase.

DIAGONAL INLAYS OF SILVER WIRE

In this project, all the wire is inlaid in a direction different from the plane of the rotation, so all the grooves must be cut by hand.

The starting point is a blackwood vase 110mm ($4\frac{5}{16}$in) high, with a shoulder width of 73mm ($2\frac{7}{8}$in) and a foot width of approximately 34mm ($1\frac{3}{8}$in) (see Fig 2.39). Note that the vase is still attached to the faceplate. In this example, the entire length of the blank was required, so it was first glued to some scrap wood to avoid wastage. An overhang has been created at the foot in order to be able to cut all the way down with the hacksaw.

MATERIALS AND METHOD

Silver wire 0.8mm (0.0315in) thick

1   Mark out a series of six equidistant dots at the base, the shoulder and the foot of the vase. In Fig 2.40 silver ink has been used for clarity. An indexing ring is helpful, although not essential.

2   Draw lines to join up these dots, thereby dividing the vase into six equal, curved segments (see Fig 2.41). (Although six lines have been used here, the procedure will work equally well with a larger number.) The lines in this example have been drawn in a curved fashion. The steepness of the curve is not

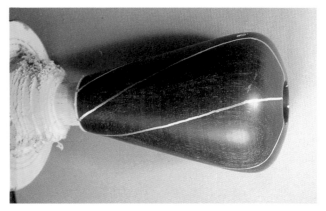

FIG 2.41
Join up the dots with curved lines.

FIG 2.42
Embed silver wire in the grooves, then sand and polish.

FIG 2.43
The finished vase, complete with diagonal inlays of silver wire and cast pewter rim and foot (see page 33).

important and can be adjusted for individual preference. Likewise, straight lines could be used instead, if preferred.

3   Using a mini-hacksaw, cut along the lines to produce grooves of the required width and depth in the usual way.

4   Inlay the silver wire in the grooves in the usual way. Sand, and then polish with metal polish (see Fig 2.42).

In this example, a metal rim made from cast pewter was attached to the neck of the vase for final decoration, and a similar pewter-cast foot was added in the final stages. Fig 2.43 shows the finished piece. The method for making the pewter rim and base is described in Chapter 3.

SILVER WIRE INLAID ALONG THE GRAIN OF A LAMP BASE

In this project, a special cutting technique is used to form an irregular groove which follows the pattern of the wood grain. Any wood which has a pronounced grain pattern can be used, regardless of whether the pattern is essentially of colour or of texture. Oak was chosen for this particular project, not only because of its grain pattern but also because I wanted the wood to be very dark in colour in order to contrast with the silver wire. To achieve this, I chose to exploit the natural tannin content in the oak to turn it a rich blue-black (see Chapter 5 for details).

SPECIAL TOOLS

A miniature electric precision drill is required for this cutting technique. A number of manufacturers make these drill kits, and prices vary enormously. The Minicraft range (made by Black & Decker) seems to be very good value, and they supply a range of these kits in various sizes and specifications.

These drills are extremely versatile tools, since a variety of attachments can be used including miniature sanding discs, burrs, cutters and small conventional drill bits. For delicate work, where a normal-size drill would be too cumbersome, these are ideal. The model I use is a particularly small version with a single speed of 16,000 rpm (see Fig 2.44). For the groove-cutting work described here I insert a small glass-engraving cutter into the collet (see Fig 2.45). The head of the engraving cutter makes a groove of just under 1mm ($\frac{1}{32}$in) – ideal for the 0.8mm (0.0315) wire which I use.

The starting point for this project is an oak lamp base 155mm ($6\frac{1}{8}$in) high, which is 85mm ($3\frac{5}{16}$in) at the widest part of the shoulder, narrowing to 40mm ($1\frac{5}{8}$in) just above the base. The base width is 72mm ($2\frac{7}{8}$in). A 10mm ($\frac{3}{8}$in) hole has been drilled through from top to bottom to take the electric flex. At this point the lamp base has not yet been parted off, but is still attached to the lathe chuck (see Fig 2.46).

MATERIALS AND METHOD

Silver wire, 0.8mm (0.0315in) thick

1   Using a solution of iron filings and vinegar, stain the wood black (see Chapter 5 for details of this staining procedure).

2   With the lathe stationary, use the miniature drill to cut along the chosen grain lines. Not all the grain lines need to be cut, and you will need to be selective. In Fig 2.47, four lines

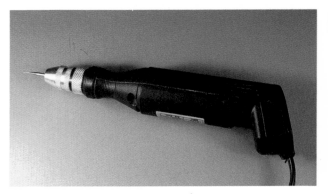

FIG 2.44
A miniature precision drill – a versatile tool for use in decorating woodturned items.

FIG 2.46
Starting point: an oak lamp base, still attached to the lathe chuck.

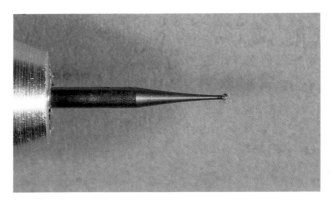

FIG 2.45
A small glass-engraving cutter, ideal for making inlay grooves along grain lines.

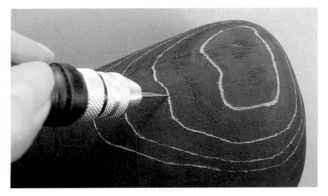

FIG 2.47
Cut grooves along selected grain lines, using the miniature drill and glass-engraving cutter.

were chosen. As always, try to ensure that the depth of the cut is appropriate and consistent along the entire length of the groove.

TIP

It is a good idea to practise this cutting technique beforehand on some scrap wood. It is not easy at first and requires a very steady hand. With practice and patience, however, a reasonably smooth cut can be obtained.

3 When the grooves have been cut to the correct depth, embed the silver wire in the usual way (see Fig 2.48) and sand. It is possible that some of the black stain may be sanded away, revealing the natural colour of the oak. These patches can be re-stained easily and quickly by applying more vinegar and iron-filings solution. (Alternatively, you could stain the lamp base *after* embedding the wire, in order to

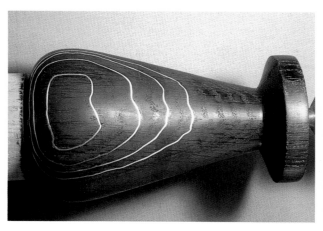

FIG 2.48
Embed silver wire in the grooves.

avoid retouching. In this example, I chose to stain the lamp base first, so that the cut grooves would be more clearly visible in the photographs.)

4 Apply your preferred finish. For the lamp base shown here, a light coat of sanding sealer was applied, cut back and then buffed to a soft sheen.

Fig 2.49 shows the finished piece.

FINAL NOTE

Very occasionally the inlaid wire may become slightly unseated in places after a period of a few weeks. The wire appears to 'expand' out of the groove for a distance of about 1–2mm ($\frac{1}{32}$–$\frac{1}{16}$in). I believe this is caused by fractional final shrinkage of the wood – usually when it has been brought indoors, into a centrally heated room for example.

This problem can be rectified by carefully cutting the peak of the wire where it has lifted from the groove and gently filing one end. The two free ends can then be re-glued into the groove so that they abut exactly. Of course, localized sanding and finishing will need to be carried out around this area afterwards, but if done carefully the repair can be almost invisible.

Although this problem only arises occasionally, it is worth keeping an item indoors for a few weeks to 'settle' and then examining it, especially if you are intending to sell it or give it away as a gift.

FIG 2.49
The completed lamp base, finished and buffed to a soft sheen.

3
MOLTEN METAL

◆ Pewter ◆ Tube-bending alloy ◆ Other low melting-point alloys ◆
◆ Casting hints ◆ Safety ◆

PROJECTS

◆ Pewter cast to embellish a vase ◆ Alloy injected into a banksia nut bud-vase ◆

ESSENTIAL EQUIPMENT

Epoxy resin glue
Basic turning tools and materials
Source of heat, e.g. cooker or portable gas stove
Old ladle
Metal can and old saucepan
10ml plastic syringe

Some of the most spectacular decorative effects can be created through the use of molten metal. In its liquid form, metal can be cast into any shape we desire, or it can be inserted into cracks and crevices in wood to create unusual and stunning effects.

Most metals have a high melting point and are therefore unsuitable for use at home or in the workshop without special equipment. However, there are some metals which have a particularly low melting point, and these are ideal since they can be melted and poured relatively easily and require no more than everyday household equipment.

The two metals used in this chapter are pewter and tube-bending alloy (sometimes called 'woods metal' or 'serrabend'). Both can be purchased from specialists suppliers, usually through mail order. Companies which supply sculpture sundries sometimes stock these metals.

PEWTER

Pewter was traditionally known as 'poor man's silver' and it does resemble silver, but with a slightly 'bluer' tone. Being much cheaper than silver, it is ideal for casting where there is always some wastage. Unlike silver, it does not tarnish.

Nowadays most stockists supply a 'lead-free' pewter, which consists mainly of tin, with some antimony and copper. It has a melting point of around 245°C and is a high-grade alloy, suitable for very detailed castings. It produces a good finish.

TUBE-BENDING ALLOY

This alloy consists of a mixture of tin, lead, cadmium and bismuth and, as its name suggests, is usually used for pipe bending. Because of its poisonous elements (lead and cadmium), care should be taken when using it.

Tube-bending alloy has an extremely low melting point of 70°C which, being lower than the boiling point of water, makes it a very versatile substance, and ideal for the use to which it has been put in the project on page 37.

OTHER LOW MELTING-POINT ALLOYS

There are many other alloys readily available through mail-order suppliers which also have very low melting points, ranging from 150°C to 290°C. They usually consist of varying proportions of tin, antimony, lead and bismuth. I prefer to use tube-bending alloy, however, because it has the lowest melting point and can be heated over boiling water, while the others cannot.

CASTING HINTS

Pouring molten metal into a mould, hole or crevice of any kind is fairly straightforward, but you must remember that although the metal is in liquid form, it does not behave like water. Air pockets form readily under the molten metal, and these must be avoided. When using a standard mould of any kind, air pockets can be eliminated by creating 'sprue holes' in the bottom of the mould, through which the trapped air can escape. When pouring molten metal into the crevices of a piece of wood, however, it is not so easy to eliminate air pockets. In this case, of course, a 'casting' as such is not required, the metal remaining in the crevices as decoration. In this sense, air pockets do not matter. However, trapped air *can* be a problem in these circumstances, because if the crevice is too shallow it will itself act as an air pocket, and the molten metal will not flow in but will sit over the surface in a blob (see Fig 3.1). Consequently, only reasonably large

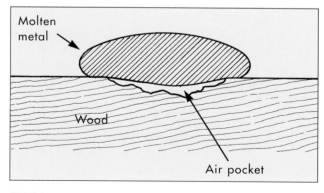

FIG 3.1
Molten metal will not flow into shallow crevices, resulting in air pockets.

crevices can be filled with molten metal in this way. Trial and error will reveal the minimum depth which will allow metal to be poured in successfully.

SAFETY

Usually, metal casting is a simple procedure and not at all dangerous. Nevertheless, as with many activities (including woodturning!), there is a small hazardous element, and it is wise to take steps to prevent potential accidents wherever possible.

When using molten metal, care should be taken at all times to avoid spillage and splashing. Always wear eye protection and protective clothing. Rubber gloves are useful for protecting hands. Finally, make sure that the worksurface is uncluttered and the workpiece is well supported.

PEWTER CAST TO EMBELLISH A VASE

In Chapter 2, we created a vase inlaid with diagonal lines of silver wire. The vase was later embellished with a rim and base made from cast pewter. This project explains how this was achieved. The starting point therefore, is the inlaid blackwood vase shown on page 28 (see Fig 2.43).

MATERIALS AND METHOD

Small pieces of pewter

1   To make a mould for the rim, mount a short piece of scrap wood on the lathe, supported at the headstock only, and rough down to a cylinder approximately 60mm (2⅜in) in diameter and 25mm (1in) long. (The method of chucking is immaterial, but it is important that the mould can be removed from the lathe and remounted.)

2   True-up the end face and cut a ring-shaped recess 14mm (½in) deep and with an outside diameter 33mm (1¼in) and an inside diameter 15mm (⅝in). (These measurements must be precise if they are to correspond to the vase dimensions in Chapter 2.)

3   Remove the scrap wood from the lathe and drill a series of small holes in the base of the recess. The depth of the holes is not critical – approximately 3mm (⅛in) is adequate. Figs 3.2 and 3.3 show the completed mould.

FIG 3.2
The scrap-wood mould for the rim, complete with sprue holes.

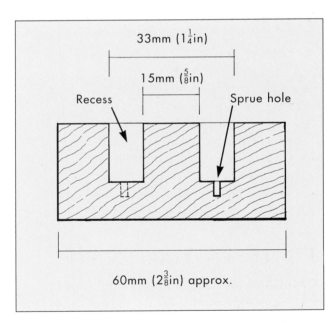

FIG 3.3
Cross section of the scrap-wood mould.

4   Place some pieces of pewter in an old ladle and place the cup of the ladle over a hot stove. After a few minutes, the pewter will begin to melt. When it is fully melted, a 'skin' will have formed on the surface. Skim this off using an old teaspoon or something similar.

33

FIG 3.4
Pour the molten pewter into the mould – it will harden quickly.

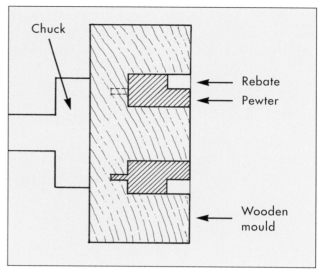

FIG 3.6
Cross-section of the rebate.

5 Pour the molten pewter into the wooden mould until reaches the surface (see Fig 3.4).

6 When the pewter has hardened and cooled, remount the mould on to the lathe, switch on, and, using a low lathe speed, true-up the end surface of the pewter.

7 Rebate the outer edge of the circle of pewter to form a spigot in the centre (see Figs 3.5 and 3.6). The diameter of the central spigot is

critical, as it is to be inserted into the neck of the vase and must be an exact fit. The diameter of the spigot should therefore be the same as the diameter of the vase neck (see Fig 3.7).

8 Using a parting tool, remove the surrounding wood from the side of the pewter casting to *almost* the depth of the original recess. In other words, expose *nearly* the entire casting. *Be careful at this point:* if you remove the wood too vigorously and too far, you run the risk of the pewter flying free from the mould, since there

FIG 3.5
Rebate the edge of the pewter to form a spigot.

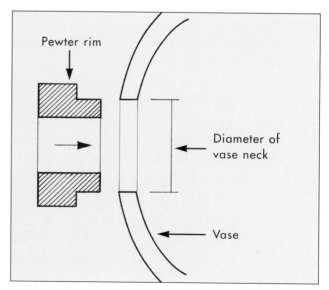

FIG 3.7
The diameter of the spigot should match that of the vase neck.

is nothing left to hold it in place. (Provided that care is taken at this stage there is no danger, because the metal in the sprue holes will help to anchor it in place.)

9 With the lathe stationary, remove the pewter casting from the mould. Remove the remains of the scrap wood from the lathe.

10 Remount the vase on the lathe and glue the pewter casting in place, inserting the spigot into the neck of the vase (see Fig 3.8). A strong glue, such as epoxy resin, is recommended.

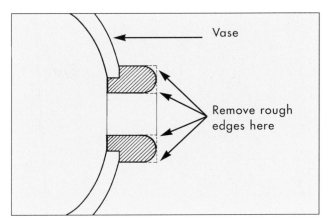

FIG 3.9
Form sweeping curves on the inner and outer edges of the rim.

FIG 3.8
Insert the spigot into the neck of the vase and glue the pewter casting in place.

FIG 3.10
Sand and polish the pewter rim to a high shine.

11 When the glue is dry, start the lathe and begin to shape the pewter rim, using whichever turning tools seem easiest and most appropriate. Remove the rough edges, to form sweeping curves on the inner and outer edges of the rim (see Fig 3.9).

12 Sand the rim, starting with 180 grit sandpaper and working through the grades up to 1,000 grit. With the lathe still running, give a final polish using ordinary metal polish applied on a soft cloth. Buff to a high shine (see Fig 3.10). Part off the vase.

13 To make a mould for the base, mount a piece of scrap wood on the lathe as before and cut a disc-shaped recess with a diameter of 39mm ($1\frac{1}{2}$in) and depth of 6mm ($\frac{1}{4}$in) (see Fig 3.11). Drill sprue holes in the base of the recess, as before.

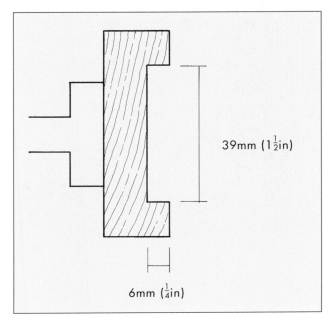

39mm ($1\frac{1}{2}$in)

6mm ($\frac{1}{4}$in)

FIG 3.11
Cut a disc-shaped rebate in the scrap wood.

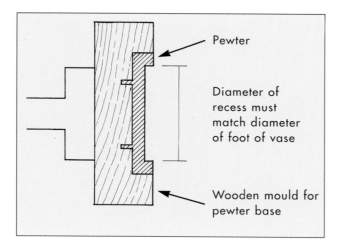

FIG 3.12
Cut a recess in the pewter casting to fit the foot of the vase.

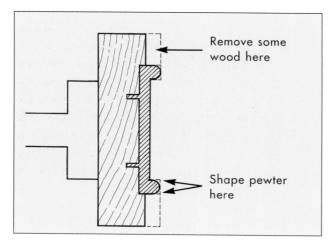

FIG 3.13
Remove some wood from the sides and shape the inner and outer edges of the pewter casting.

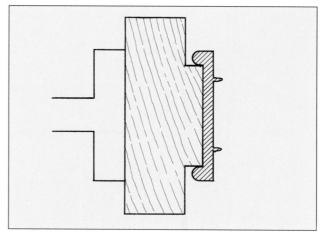

FIG 3.14
Reverse the pewter base on to the scrap-wood spigot.

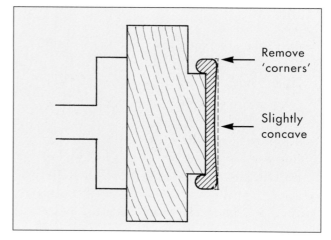

FIG 3.15
Shape the sides of the pewter base by removing the 'corners', and make the underside slightly concave.

14 Remove the mould from the lathe and pour in molten pewter as before. When the pewter is cool, remount the mould on the lathe.

15 True-up the end face of the pewter and cut a recess in the end, the diameter of which must correspond *exactly* to the foot of the vase (see Fig 3.12). In this example, it will measure approximately 32mm (1¼in).

16 Using a parting tool, remove some wood from the sides of the pewter casting and shape the inner and outer edges (see Fig 3.13). Sand and polish these edges, and remove the pewter casting from the mould.

17 Recut the mould to form a spigot with *exactly* the same diameter as the foot of the vase. Place

the half-turned pewter base over this spigot, which now acts as a spigot chuck to support it firmly, so that the underside can be turned (see Fig 3.14).

18 Shape the sides and end face of the base, forming a shallow dish shape on the bottom (see Fig 3.15).

19 Sand and polish in the same way as for the rim, then remove the pewter base from the chuck.

20 Using a strong epoxy resin, glue the pewter base on to the foot of the vase.

Fig 2.43 on page 28 shows the finished vase.

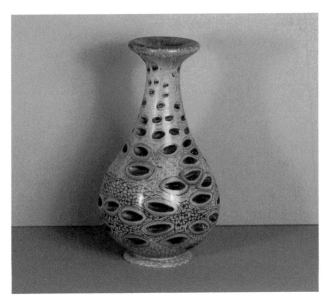

FIG 3.16
Starting point: a bud-vase turned from a banksia nut.

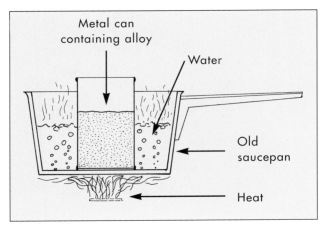

FIG 3.17
Heat the alloy in a metal can placed in a pan of boiling water.

ALLOY INJECTED INTO A BANKSIA NUT BUD-VASE

In this project, tube-bending alloy is melted over boiling water and inserted into the holes of a banksia nut, using a plastic syringe. The starting point is a bud-vase turned from a banksia nut, with a height of 120mm ($4\frac{3}{4}$in) and maximum width of 57mm ($2\frac{1}{4}$in) (see Fig 3.16).

MATERIALS AND METHOD

Small pieces of tube-bending alloy

Newspaper or old cloth

Plaster (optional)

1   Place some pieces of tube-bending alloy in a metal can, which is in turn placed in an old saucepan containing a few inches of water (see Fig 3.17).

2   Place the pan on a hot stove. While the water is heating, place the banksia nut bud-vase horizontally in a firm 'cradle' of newspaper or old cloth. This will support the vase and prevent it from rolling around, yet will also leave it free to be rotated. Place a 10ml plastic syringe in a separate container of hot water to warm it.

3   After a while, the boiling water will melt the alloy. Remove the syringe from the hot water, draw up some of the molten alloy into it and inject it into the holes in the banksia nut (see Fig 3.18). This must be done fairly quickly, before the alloy has time to harden inside the syringe. If it *does* harden, just place the nozzle of the syringe in the can of molten alloy and it will re-melt. It is not necessary to fill *all* the holes – how many will depend on personal taste and individual patience!

TIP

The holes in a banksia nut are quite deep. To prevent wastage of metal it is a good idea to plug the holes beforehand with plaster, leaving relatively shallow recesses into which the alloy can be poured. However, if the recesses are too shallow the alloy will not penetrate. In Fig 3.18 the plaster can be seen in some of the holes.

4   When all the required holes have been filled, the vase will look very messy, with excess metal protruding from the holes (see Fig 3.19). Using a small metal file, carefully file away most of the surplus metal, taking care not to damage the surface of the wood. The same effect can be achieved using a coarse grade of sandpaper. When the metal has been filed or sanded back flush with the surface, continue to sand, working through the grades and finishing with 1,000 grit.

FIG 3.18
Inject the molten alloy into selected holes in the banksia nut.

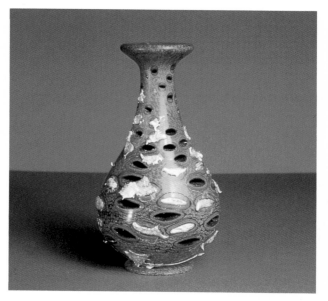

FIG 3.19
A bit messy – but this is normal for this stage, with excess alloy protruding from the holes.

imaginative use of molten metal. It is possible to create similar effects rather more easily by using casting resin mixed with metal filler. The results are not quite as good, but are nevertheless quite acceptable and very attractive. This process is described in detail in Chapter 12.

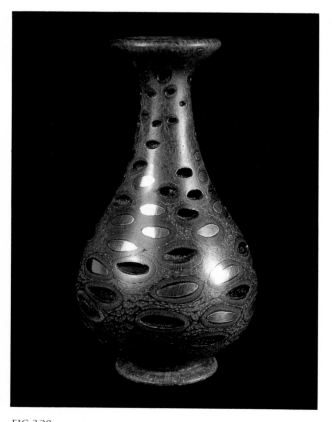

FIG 3.20
The finished vase, carefully sanded by hand – not on the lathe, which could be hazardous.

This last stage takes a very long time, since it has to be done by hand. Do *not* be tempted to remount the vase on the lathe and sand with the lathe running. After the metal has cooled it will shrink very slightly, and the centrifugal force produced by the high-speed rotation could cause some of the pieces of hardened metal to be jetti-soned from the rotating workpiece at lethal speed.

Fig 3.20 shows the finished vase. Fig 3.21 shows a natural-edged bowl made from salmon gum burr, which has had molten tube-bending alloy inserted into some of the natural crevices.

This chapter has demonstrated some of the dramatic effects which can be created with the

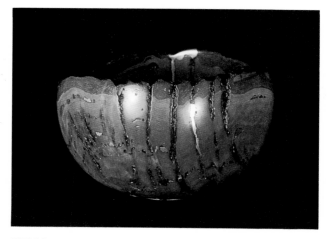

FIG 3.21
A bowl turned from salmon gum burr, with molten alloy injected into some of the natural crevices.

4
LAMINATING
WITH SHEET METAL

◆ Selection of sheet metal ◆ Design considerations ◆ Safety ◆

PROJECTS

◆ Small laminated platter ◆ Laminated bud-vase ◆

ESSENTIAL EQUIPMENT

Bandsaw
Strong epoxy resin glue
Basic turning tools and materials

Wood can be laminated in a variety of different ways to produce a range of effects. The projects in this chapter demonstrate just two possibilities – faceplate turning with lateral laminates, and spindle turning with longitudinal laminates – to transform a small, simple platter and bud-vase into something a bit special.

SELECTION OF SHEET METAL

Sheet metal purchased from craft shops is normally available in aluminium, copper and brass (see Fig 4.1). Which type to select for any given project will depend largely on the timber being used, the usual factors of relative colour and hardness of the metal and timber being taken into consideration.

Sheet metal is sold in a variety of thicknesses, the thickness selected for any particular project depending on the size of the object to be made, the overall design and personal taste. I usually choose 1mm ($\frac{1}{32}$ in) thick.

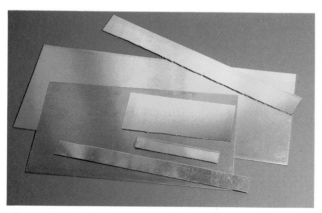

FIG 4.1
Sheet metal is normally available in aluminium, copper and brass, in a variety of thicknesses.

DESIGN CONSIDERATIONS

There are several different options for laminating wood with sheet metal.

In spindle turning, a rectangular blank might have the laminates running lengthways, parallel to the direction of the grain. These are longitudinal

laminates (see Fig 4.2). Alternatively, the laminates can run diagonally, producing a rather different effect (see Fig 4.3).

In faceplate turning, the laminates can run longitudinally (see Fig 4.4) or laterally (see Fig 4.5).

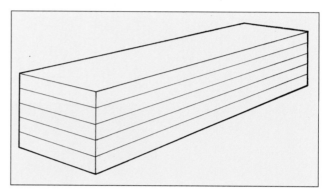

FIG 4.2
Longitudinal laminates (spindle turning).

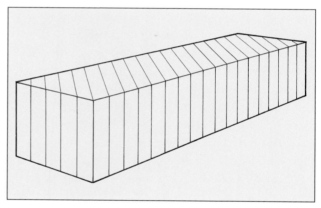

FIG 4.3
Diagonal laminates (spindle turning).

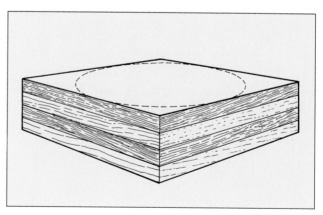

FIG 4.4
Longitudinal laminates (faceplate turning).

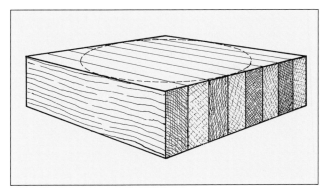

FIG 4.5
Lateral laminates (faceplate turning).

SMALL LAMINATED PLATTER

The starting point for this project is a purpleheart bowl-blank 25mm (1in) deep, with a diameter of 210mm ($8\frac{1}{4}$in). Also required is a piece of aluminium sheet measuring 254mm (10in) long, 100mm (4in) wide and approximately 1mm ($\frac{1}{32}$in) thick. This particular timber was chosen to provide a good colour contrast to the aluminium laminate (see Fig 4.6).

In addition, there are many possibilities for forming complex combinations and variations of these basic methods.

SAFETY

Laminating with sheet metal is very similar in principle to laminating with wood veneer. However, the most important thing to remember is that the type of adhesive is extremely important. Always choose one with a *high strength* and which will bond *both wood and metal*. A strong epoxy resin glue will work satisfactorily, but do make sure that it is given time to work – *never* be impatient and proceed with the turning of a laminated blank before the required setting time of the adhesive.

It is also important to abrade the surface of the metal sheet before bonding it to the wood. This provides a 'key' for the adhesive, and failure to do this can result in inadequate bonding. Warming the metal sheet before bonding can also help the adhesion.

It is imperative that these steps are followed, because when the laminated blank is rotating at high speed on the lathe, the centrifugal forces will tend to force the layers apart. A faulty bond could therefore have lethal consequences. A further safety recommendation is that the lathe speed should be slightly slower than you might normally choose.

FIG 4.6
Starting point: purpleheart bowl-blank and aluminium sheet, chosen for their contrasting colours.

MATERIALS AND METHOD

Aluminium sheet, 1mm ($\frac{1}{32}$ in) thick

1   Using a ruler and pencil, draw three lines on the bowl-blank to indicate the positions of the metal laminates. In this example they are 13mm ($\frac{1}{2}$in) apart, the line nearest the centre being 20mm ($\frac{3}{4}$in) away from the centre point. Cut along these lines using a bandsaw (see Fig 4.7).

2   Sand the sides of each piece of wood completely flat. Any unevenness on the surfaces will result in gaps when the wood is joined to the metal.

3   Saw the aluminium sheet into three strips, each 25mm (1in) wide (i.e. equal to the depth of the bowl-blank). Abrade both surfaces of each strip with a file or coarse sandpaper.

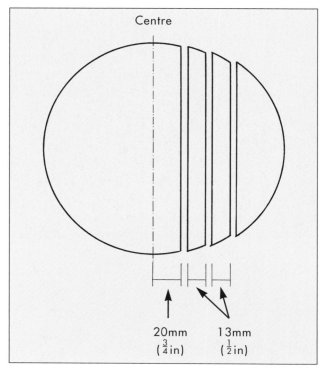

FIG 4.7
Cut along the three lines in the bowl-blank as shown.

FIGS 4.9
The faceplate fitted prior to turning.

4   Using strong epoxy resin, glue the strips of aluminium sheet in place between the cut segments of the bowl-blank (see Fig 4.8) and clamp until the glue has set. Remove any excess metal from around the edges, using tin snips or a file, as appropriate.

FIG 4.10
True-up the end face of the bowl-blank cylinder.

5   Attach a faceplate to the back of the bowl-blank, ready for mounting on the lathe (see Fig 4.9).

6   With the lathe turning, rough down the bowl-blank to a cylinder and true-up the end face (see Fig 4.10).

7   Turn the underside of the platter and sand in the usual way, finishing with 1,000 grit sandpaper. Apply any preferred finish. In this example, melamine and carnauba wax were used (see Fig 4.11).

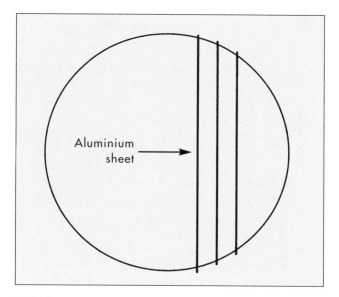

FIG 4.8
Glue the strips of aluminium sheet in position between the pieces of the bowl-blank.

8   Reverse-chuck the platter to turn the inside, then sand and finish as before.

Fig 4.12 shows the finished platter.

FIG 4.11
Turn the underside of the platter, and then sand and apply any preferred finish.

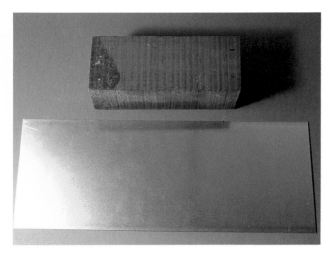

FIG 4.13
Starting point: padauk blank and aluminium sheet.

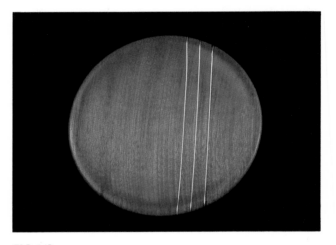

FIG 4.12
The finished platter, showing a good contrast between metal laminate and wood.

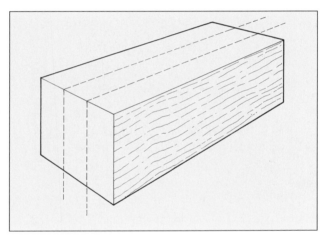

FIG 4.14
Cut the rectangular blank lengthways into three equal pieces.

LAMINATED BUD-VASE

The starting point for this project is a padauk blank 140mm (5½in) long, with a cross-section 50mm (2in) square, and a piece of aluminium sheet large enough to be cut into two equal strips, each corresponding to the length and width of the padauk (see Fig 4.13).

MATERIALS AND METHOD

Aluminium sheet, 1mm ($\frac{1}{32}$ in) thick

1 Using a bandsaw, cut the blank lengthways into three equal pieces (see Fig 4.14).

2 Sand the sawn side of each piece until completely smooth.

3 Cut the aluminium sheet into two pieces, each measuring 140 x 50mm (5½ x 2in).

4 Using strong epoxy resin, glue the aluminium sheet into position between the slices of padauk and clamp until the glue has set (see Fig 4.15).

5 Any appropriate method of chucking can be used, but because the prepared blank in this example was fairly small, I chose to glue it to the centre of a wooden faceplate.

FIG 4.15
Glue the aluminium sheets in between the slices of padauk.

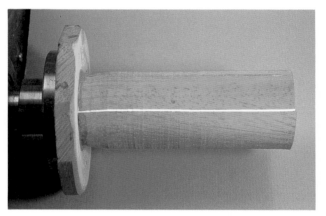

FIG 4.16
Rough down the padauk-and-aluminium blank to a cylinder.

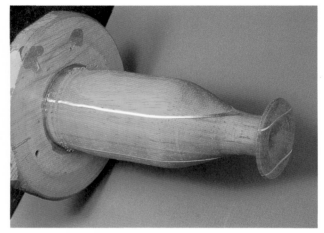

FIG 4.17
As the vase is shaped, the laminates begin to form an interesting pattern.

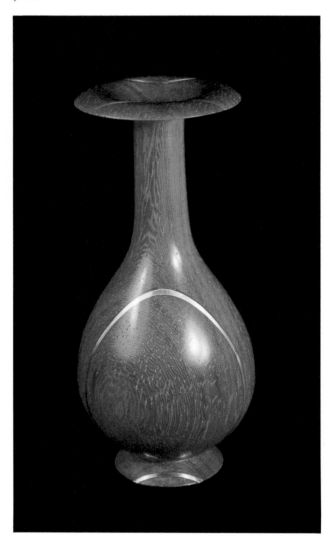

FIG 4.18
The completed vase, sanded and finished with sanding sealer and carnauba wax.

6   Rough down the blank to a cylinder (see Fig 4.16).

7   With a drill mounted in a Jacobs chuck attached to the tailstock, drill a hole approximately 10mm ($\frac{3}{8}$in) in diameter down through the centre of the cylinder. *Remember to keep the lathe speed to a minimum while drilling.*

8   Proceed to shape the vase. As can be seen in Fig 4.17, the laminates begin to take on a more interesting pattern as the bud-vase is shaped.

9   Finish the shaping and then sand the vase, finishing with 1,000 grit sandpaper. Apply any preferred finish. In this example, sanding sealer and carnauba wax were used.

Fig 4.18 shows the finished bud-vase.

PART TWO
COLOURING WOOD

Dyes and Stains

Waxes and Pastes

Inks and Paints

Gilding

INTRODUCTION

For many years there has been a great deal of controversy over whether or not wood should be coloured. The common arguments against it are:

- Colouring wood in some way detracts from its natural beauty and therefore degrades it.

I can appreciate this viewpoint. Certainly, in the majority of cases there is probably no 'need' to colour wood, because so many natural timbers already have a delightful colour which is unsurpassed by anything which could be achieved by the hand of man. Indeed, with many timbers it would be sacrilege to attempt to hide their natural beauty, which should be there for all to see.

Nevertheless, there also exist some timbers which are very plain in colour and which can be enhanced by the addition of some subtle colouring. After all, cabinet makers have been staining wood for centuries to enhance the colour or to make it resemble a different timber. Some people may feel that this is different – that it is somehow 'acceptable' to stain wood as long as you are staining it a different shade of brown!

- Wood should not be stained because in doing so you are rendering it 'unlike wood' in some way and making it resemble a different medium, such as plastic.

I think this view has come about through confusing 'staining' with 'painting'. Certainly, when wood is painted it often loses its characteristic features, notably its grain pattern, which distinguish it from other materials. This is because paint is opaque and will tend to obscure the grain. Stains and dyes, on the other hand, tend to be transparent and will not hide the grain. Indeed, the growth rings in the timber can very often be *emphasized* by the use of a stain. This is because the growth ring patterns consist of bands of fibres of different density and porosity, and this differential is enhanced by staining because of the different rates of absorption of the dye.

- Colouring wood makes it look cheap and artificial.

It certainly *can* do. The above viewpoint is formed mainly through having seen badly coloured wood, of which there are many examples. The worst I have seen use colours which are unnatural and garish, the user often applying the dye straight from the bottle without blending colours, and with little thought as to the tone and hue.

The most attractive examples I have seen use colours which are subtle and look 'believable'. By this I mean colours which are natural looking, and could almost be the real colour. That is not to say that they have to be shades of brown – I have seen examples of wood stained with a subtle grey-blue that looks extremely natural.

STEPS TO SUCCESSFUL COLOURING

For those who wish to experiment with staining wood, here are some guidelines.

- First of all, ask yourself *why* you want to colour a given piece of wood or woodturned item. Is it because you want to highlight the grain pattern? Is it because the wood you have selected is rather dull in colour? Or do you simply want to create something which looks a little different? Whatever the reason, think carefully about the type of colour you wish to create. What shade and tone should it be? Will it complement the texture of the wood? Do you want the object to be a uniform colour all over, or do you want to blend the colour in some parts? The planning stage is, as always, as important as the implementation. Colouring wood is not simply a case of slapping on the colour – you *can* do it this way, but unless you are lucky, you are likely to be less than satisfied with the results.

- Try various different brands of dye. Some manufacturers produce wood dyes which have very attractive, natural colours, while others produce shades which in my opinion, are hideous. It would be unfortunate to be put off through having only used one of the latter!

- Never use dyes straight from the bottle. Mix them to produce different shades – the colours you get in this way will, very probably, be better. It is also wise to dilute them: colours which are too strong can look artificial (the exception here, perhaps, is black, unless a charcoal grey is desired).

- Try to create natural-looking, subtle shades. These will usually look best.

- Use transparent dyes, which do not obscure the grain of the wood.

Remember that these are guidelines only, not hard-and-fast rules, and there are always exceptions. For example, there are occasions when a bright colour is required – one which is neither natural nor subtle. It might be chosen to match a piece of furniture or fabric, or simply because the user likes that colour and thinks it looks attractive. That is fine. Experiment and be bold.

Similarly, although I have stated earlier that paints are less desirable because they obscure the grain, there are occasions when paint (notably black), can be used to good effect, and an example of this is given in Chapter 7.

INKS, PAINTS AND OTHER COLOURANTS

So far, we have considered mainly dyes and stains. These are perhaps the most common methods for colouring wood. However, other substances can also be used, such as inks, paints, pastes, waxes, powders and varnishes.

Paints and inks can be very useful for colouring small areas, such as the rims and bases of bowls. Black Indian Ink and metallic inks, in particular, can be used to good effect. Coloured waxes and pastes are produced specifically for use on wood. Many people are familiar with liming wax, for example, which can be very attractive when used on coarse-grained woods. Black patinating wax can be used in the same way, in some instances creating an almost 'antique' effect. A whole range of other coloured and metallic pastes is also available, which can give an interesting and unusual lustre to the surface of the wood. Finally, metallic powders and varnishes can be useful for gilding wooden objects. With all these products, however, the best results are usually obtained if they are used sparingly – to cover a small, localized area, perhaps.

Above all, in the realm of wood colouring, experimentation is the key. If you think it might work, try it and see.

5
DYES AND STAINS

◆ Selecting dyes and stains ◆ Fabric dyes ◆ Light fastness ◆ Home-made dyes ◆
◆ Tannin ◆ Ebonizing and bleaching ◆ General principles ◆

PROJECTS

◆ Tulipwood bowl stained with logwood dye ◆
◆ Burr oak bowl stained with tannin and silk dye ◆ Elm platter stained with silk dyes ◆
◆ Ebonized oak bowl ◆

ESSENTIAL EQUIPMENT

Selection of paintbrushes and cloths
Cleaning solvent
Rubber gloves
Wire wool
Basic turning tools and materials

In the introduction to this section I used the words 'dye' and 'stain' interchangeably. Strictly speaking, it is incorrect to do so, because they are not quite the same thing and they differ in their mode of operation. Broadly speaking, a stain forms a chemical reaction with the wood, causing the latter to change colour, while dyes work by imparting tiny particles of pigment permanently to the wood. On the whole, stains tend to be more permanent and light fast then dyes, although there are some dyes which hold their colour extremely well over long periods of time.

The different between stains and dyes, then, is largely a technical one. Luckily, for our purposes the distinction is unimportant, since it is the end result which is our main concern.

SELECTING DYES AND STAINS

Dyes and stains usually come in one of three forms.

Water-based dyes and stains are perhaps the most versatile, because they are compatible with any finish. They do take a little longer to apply, however, because, being water-based, they raise the grain on application. To prevent this happening, the grain must be raised *before* applying the dye, by wetting the wood with cold water, letting it dry thoroughly and then cutting it back lightly with fine-grade abrasive. Before applying the dye, wet the wood *again* and apply the dye to the wet wood to enable it to impregnate evenly. If you apply a water-based dye directly to dry wood, you sometimes get brushmarks where darker 'overlaps' are visible. (This can happen regardless of whether you use a brush or a cloth.)

Spirit-based dyes and stains do not raise the grain of the wood, and can be applied directly to dry wood. However, they are a little less versatile than water-based types because they cannot be used under a spirit-based finish, such as sanding sealer or melamine, as this will tend to dissolve the dye.

Oil-based dyes and stains can be used in a similar way to spirit-based ones. However, they are *not* compatible with an oil-based finish.

Some wood dyes come ready prepared in diluted liquid form and can be used straight from the bottle, if desired. Others come in concentrated liquid form and should be diluted before use. Yet others are available in powder form and must be dissolved in water or spirit before they can be used. Although this is more time-consuming, it can prove a more economical way of buying dyes.

Which type of dye or stain you choose will depend partly upon the colour range available in any particular brand, your personal taste leading you to certain brands rather than others. Another important factor to consider is the type of finish you want. As explained above, an oil-based stain cannot be used with an oil-based finish, and a spirit-based stain cannot be used with a spirit-based finish. I therefore usually choose water-based stains and dyes, because they can be used under any finish.

If you do have problems finding a compatible finish for an item after staining, it is worth using spray-on melamine. Since this is sprayed on lightly rather than being applied with a cloth, it does not dissolve and wipe away the colour underneath. If you prefer a matt finish, the melamine can be cut back after drying using wire wool, to produce a less glossy surface.

FABRIC DYES

Many forms of fabric dye can also be used very successfully on wood, and in many cases the colours are nicer than proprietary wood dyes. There are a great many different types of fabric dye, and some will work better on wood than others: trial and error will reveal the most successful brands.

Those dyes which require the fabric to be boiled in the dye can be applied hot to the wood. When dyeing wood, there is no need to apply the usual fixer after dyeing, because it is mainly needed to prevent the colour washing out of fabric. However, it must be remembered that the fixer also helps to prevent the colour from fading after long-term exposure to light.

I very often use silk dyes on wood, since the colours are good and the dye is absorbed well.

LIGHT FASTNESS

Dyes vary in their degree of light fastness. Some are very light fast and will not fade readily; others will fade after relatively short exposure to light. With dyes which have been produced specifically for wood, the light fastness has been tested and is usually very good. With fabric dyes, however, the light fastness on wood is not guaranteed, so trial and error will be needed to prove which brands are the most successful in this respect. When experimenting with different brands, leave finished dyed items on a sunny windowsill for a while and see how readily they fade.

It is important to remember, however, that even the most light-fast dyes – be they applied to wood, fabric or whatever – are not 100% light fast, and in time most colours will fade to a certain extent. Sunlight treats all colours harshly, so it is wise to store or display finished items away from direct sunlight.

HOME-MADE DYES

So far we have only considered commercial dyes of one kind or another. Certainly, these are the most reliable, the easiest to use, and the least messy and time consuming. However, for those who enjoy a challenge and who like trying something different, it can be fun to make dyes using natural products.

Before the introduction of chemical-based dyes in the nineteenth century, most dyestuffs were indeed made from natural products – flowers, fruits and berries, vegetables, lichens, tree bark, minerals and so on. Woad, indigo and madder are all dyes which have ancient origins, and some of these have been used for thousands of years for dyeing fibres such as wool, silk, cotton and flax (linen).

MORDANTS

Some dyestuffs require a mordant to be mixed with them. This is a substance which helps to 'fix' the dye. Mordants are not absolutely necessary when dyeing wood, although they can sometimes help to improve light fastness. When dyeing fabrics the mordant is applied to the fabric before the application of the dye; when dyeing wood, however, the mordant can be mixed with the dye itself. An interesting aspect of mordants is that they often change the colour of the dye, different mordants producing different colours with the same dye.

Mordants are usually acidic or alkaline, or contain some metallic extract, such as iron. White vinegar, lemon juice, water in which wire wool has been left to soak (for the iron content) and cold, strong black tea (for the tannin content) can all act as natural mordants. Modern chemical alternatives include the following salts: alum (potassium aluminium sulphate); cream of tartar (potassium hydrogen tartrate); baking soda (sodium bicarbonate); washing soda (sodium carbonate); baking powder (a mixture of baking soda and cream of tartar). These can be purchased from chemists or supermarkets. They can be mixed together to produce further colour changes to the dye.

NATURAL DYESTUFFS

Turmeric When boiled in water, this powder produces a brown liquid which gives a very strong, bright yellow colour to wood.

Onion skins When boiled in water for an hour so, skins from brown onions produce an attractive golden orange colour. Red onions produce a coral-pink shade.

Cochineal Nowadays, it can be difficult to acquire 'real' cochineal (originally made from beetles), but artificial cochineal – a common red food colouring – is freely available and works well. It can be applied directly to the wood or diluted first. It gives a good strong red colour.

Logwood This comes from a Central American tree (*Haematoxylon campechianum*) and has been used as a dyestuff for centuries. Timber merchants who stock timber for woodturners will sometimes sell it. Fig 5.1 shows a small bowl made from logwood and a pile of the woodshavings: if you are able to acquire any, it is worth buying because it turns beautifully, has a deep red colour, and you can keep the shavings if you so wish for making dye.

The shavings are boiled in water for a couple of hours, and the resultant dark liquid strained off and kept as a dye base. Many different colours can be made from one batch of the solution, depending on the mordant used. Fig 5.2 shows some samples of dyed wood, all using the same logwood dye base but with different mordants.

FIG 5.1
A logwood bowl and shavings, useful for making dye.

The above examples of natural dyestuffs represent only a fraction of the possibilities. Berries, lichens, tree barks and so on can yield some good dyes but not all such substances will. Very often, an item which is very vivid in its natural colour, and which you think ought to yield a good dye, can be disappointing. Conversely, some excellent dyes can be obtained from unlikely sources. Trial and error alone will reveal the most successful. Always remember to test for light fastness when trying out new dyes.

FIG 5.2
Samples dyed using the same logwood base, but different mordants. Each joined 'pair' of cylinders shows the dye without finish (left) and with sanding sealer finish (right). From left to right, the mordants used were: (top row) none; alum; washing soda; (bottom row) baking soda; baking powder; alum + iron filings and white vinegar solution.

Fig 5.3 shows a set of wooden apples, each dyed with a different 'natural' dye.

FIG 5.3
Wooden 'apples', each dyed with a different natural dye. From left to right, the dyes and mordants used were: turmeric with alum; cochineal, no mordant; logwood with alum; red onion skin with cream of tartar; brown onion skin with alum and cream of tartar.

TANNIN

Tannin is a chemical compound which occurs naturally in certain hardwoods (broad-leaved, deciduous trees). Not all hardwoods contain tannin, and of those which do, there is considerable variation in the amount they contain. The timber which is perhaps best known for its tannin content is oak. Oak bark used to be harvested for use in the leather-tanning process, since tannin has a preservative effect on animal proteins.

Tannin reacts with iron and water to produce a deep blue-black stain. Some people may have observed this effect in old oak posts, where rain has reacted with iron nails to produce a black stain.

Other timbers which contain tannin include acacia (tannin-rich), walnut and yew (moderate amounts). To discover whether a particular timber contains a significant amount of tannin, simply rub the surface with a solution of iron filings and white vinegar. The extent to which the wood turns black (if at all) is an indication of its tannin content.

USING TANNIN

The occurrence of tannin in certain timbers is useful for those wishing to stain wood a natural black without the use of commercial dyes or stains. The procedure is very simple.

1   Make a solution of iron filings and vinegar and leave for several days. If you cannot obtain iron filings, rusty nails or wire wool can be used instead.

2   Rub the solution into the surface of the wood using wire wool. The abrasive property of the wire wool serves to cut back the raised grain as it appears, so there is no need to wet the wood to raise the grain beforehand, as with water-based dyes. A deep black stain will be produced almost immediately.

An alternative method is simply to rub water into the surface of the wood using a piece of wire wool. The same effect will be produced, but it will take much longer. (The acid in the white vinegar acts as a catalyst to the chemical reaction, while the iron filings produce a more concentrated solution).

Any finish may be applied after the wood has dried.

TIP

Because tannin will react so readily with iron and water to produce a black stain, this should be remembered before applying water-based dyes to wood. Do not use wire wool to cut back raised grain prior to applying the dye, because tiny particles of the wool can become embedded in the wood fibres, and the iron content of the wire wool may react with the tannin in the presence of water, creating tiny black specks. This will not occur in timbers which are tannin free, of course, but if in doubt it is better to cut back using a fine grade of abrasive paper.

EBONIZING AND BLEACHING

Ebonizing is a rather grand term for blackening wood. It does not necessarily mean that the finished item looks like ebony – although it might do, depending on the method used and the type of timber.

Wood can be blackened by using standard stains or dyes, by using the wood's natural tannin content in certain cases, and even by scorching it. Fig 5.4

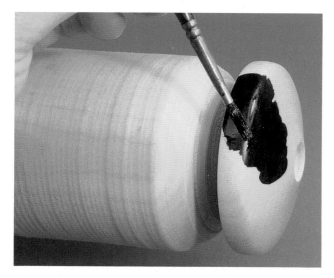

FIG 5.4
'Ebonizing' the base of a candlestick using black spirit-based dye.

shows the base of a holly candlestick being 'ebonized' by the application of spirit-based black dye. The finished candlestick is shown in Fig 5.5.

Bleaching simply refers to the removal of some of the wood's natural colour in order to make it paler. It is rarely necessary to bleach wood, because it is easier to use a pale-coloured timber to begin with, but there are occasions when you might want to use a bleaching technique, either because a pale timber is not available, or because you wish to create an item that is almost white. Occasionally, bleach may also be used to lighten localized darker areas of wood.

Bleaching can be carried out by applying a solution of hydrogen peroxide and sodium hydroxide to the surface of the wood, leaving it to dry, and then applying a neutralizing solution of white vinegar. However, more consistent results can be obtained by using a commercial wood bleach, and this is the method I would certainly recommend.

When using bleaches, always wear rubber gloves, and protect your eyes and clothing from splashes. Figs 5.6 and 5.7 show a sycamore vase before and after bleaching with a commercial bleach.

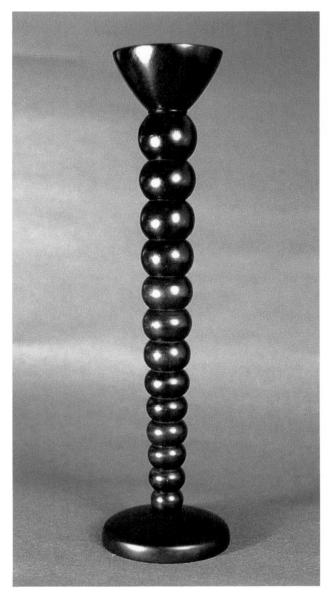

FIG 5.5
The finished, ebonized candlestick.

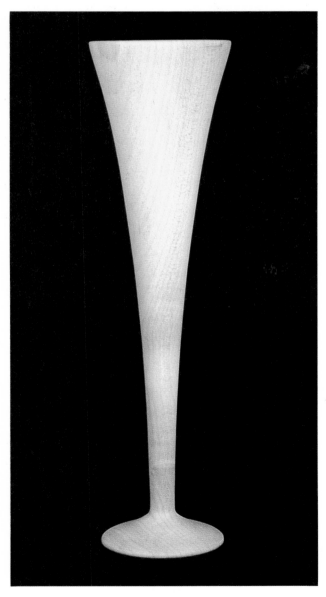

FIG 5.6
A sycamore vase before bleaching . . .

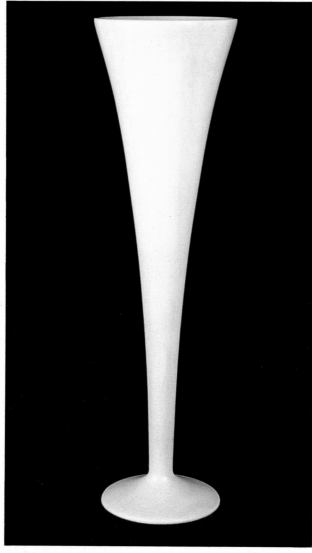

FIG 5.7
. . . and after bleaching.

GENERAL PRINCIPLES

There are a number of general points which apply to all methods of staining and dyeing wood.

First and foremost do test a sample of the selected dye or stain on a piece of scrap wood. This is essential, because the end result can often be very different from what you expected. However, it is important to ensure that the test piece is identical in every way to the item you intend to stain. It should be the same wood, sanded to the same extent, using the same dilution of dye applied to both side and end grains. The reasons for this are:

- Any given dye will produce slightly different effects on different timbers. The density, porosity and oiliness of the wood all affect its receptivity to dye. The base colour of the wood will also determine the final shade.

- Different concentrations of the dye solution can produce slightly different colour shades.

- The dye will create a darker shade on coarsely sanded wood, and a lighter shade on finely sanded wood.

- Likewise, end grain – being more porous and absorbent – will be rendered darker than side grain. Items which have both side grain and end grain (e.g. bowls) will vary in tone gradually around the circumference, becoming darker towards the areas of end grain and paler towards areas of side grain. Provided the dye has been applied evenly, these tonal variations do not matter – indeed, they enhance the appearance and show off the grain features to best effect.

It is also important to remember that any finish applied to wood on top of dye will cause the colour to change slightly, so always apply your chosen finish to the test piece and leave it to dry thoroughly before inspecting the final effect.

If you are planning to do a lot of wood dyeing, it is a good idea to build up a 'bank' of test samples, labelled clearly with the type of dye used and its concentration, the timber used, and the finish applied. This is very helpful for future reference.

It is a common misconception that stains and dyes will cover up defects and blemishes on the surface of the wood. Unlike paint, which is opaque, dyes and stains are transparent, so they do not hide surface defects. On the contrary, they *emphasize* them. This is because sanding marks, rough patches and other scratches are more porous than the surrounding wood, absorb the dye more readily and are revealed as darker patches on the surface. Because of this, wood which is dyed must be absolutely scratch free, and you must therefore be scrupulous with the sanding.

TULIPWOOD BOWL STAINED WITH LOGWOOD DYE

The starting point for this project is a half-turned bowl made from European tulipwood. The dimensions are: height 65mm ($2\frac{1}{2}$in), width at rim 140mm ($5\frac{1}{2}$in), width at foot 40mm ($1\frac{5}{8}$in). The underside has been turned, and the bowl is still attached to the screw-chuck. The surface of the wood should be finely sanded and checked for any rough patches (see Fig 5.8).

MATERIALS AND METHOD

Logwood shavings

Selected mordant

1   Prepare the dye base by simmering logwood shavings in water for two hours and straining the resulting solution. Add a very small quantity of the desired mordant. Baking powder was used here.

2   Wet the surface of the wood with water to raise the grain. Leave to dry and then cut back using fine abrasive cloth, not wire wool.

3   Wet the surface again to ensure even coverage of the dye.

4   With the surface of the wood still wet, apply the hot solution to the surface of the bowl (see Fig 5.9) – hot liquid is more readily absorbed than cold.

5   Leave the wood to dry completely. Apply a second coat of dye until the colour is even throughout.

6   Apply the desired finish. In this example, sanding sealer and wax were used.

7   Reverse-chuck the bowl and turn the inside. Sand finely.

8   Repeat steps 2–6 with the inside of the bowl.

Fig 5.10 shows the finished bowl.

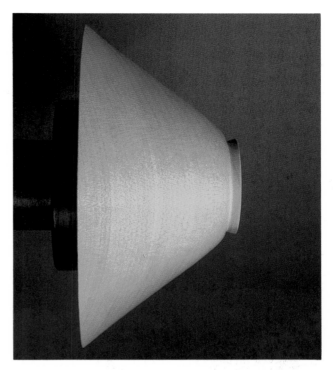

FIG 5.8
Starting point: tulipwood bowl.

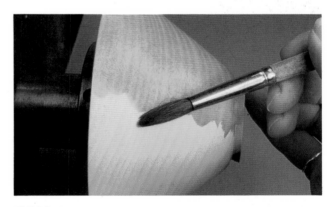

FIG 5.9
Apply hot logwood dye to the surface of the bowl.

FIG 5.10
The completed bowl, finished with sanding sealer and wax.

FIG 5.11
Starting point: a piece of burr oak.

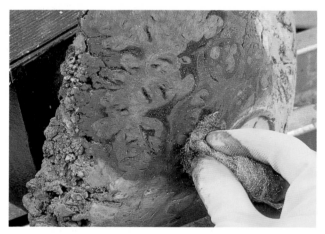

FIG 5.12
Apply iron filings and white vinegar solution to the surface using a pad of wire wool.

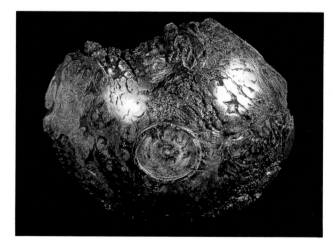

FIG 5.13
The underside of the bowl, finished with sanding sealer and carnauba wax.

BURR OAK BOWL STAINED WITH TANNIN AND SILK DYE

The inspiration for this particular piece came from examining semi-precious mineral stones in their raw state. I was attracted by the rough outer surface contrasting with the highly coloured, jewel-like crystals within. I attempted to create a similar effect with a piece of burr oak, leaving the outer surface highly textured and dark, with the inside paler, coloured and highly polished.

The starting point for this project is an oak burr of maximum width 240mm ($9\frac{1}{2}$in) and depth 35mm ($1\frac{3}{8}$in) (see Fig 5.11).

MATERIALS AND METHOD

White vinegar and iron filings solution

Blue-green water-based silk dye

1 Prepare a solution of iron filings and white vinegar and leave for several days.

2 Attach the burr to the lathe and turn the underside, cutting a recess in the base for reverse-chucking. Sand thoroughly, finishing with 400 grit sandpaper.

3 Apply the iron and vinegar solution to the wood surface using a pad of wire wool. The iron will react with the tannin in the wood to create a deep blue-black stain. Rub in thoroughly until a good even colour is achieved (see Fig 5.12).

4 When the whole of the underside has been stained, leave to dry.

5 Remove any remaining traces of raised grain using wire wool, until a smooth surface is achieved.

6 Apply the desired finish. In this example, sanding sealer was used, followed by carnauba wax (see Fig 5.13).

7 Reverse-chuck the bowl and turn the inside. Sand finely.

8 Wet the surface of the wood to raise the grain. Leave to dry and cut back.

9 Wet the surface again and apply a dilute solution of blue-green water-based dye. (In this example a silk dye was used, but any water-based dye could be chosen.) Leave to dry thoroughly.

10 With the lathe running, burnish the surface with a clean, dry cloth, then apply sanding sealer and carnauba wax, or another preferred finish.

Fig 5.14 shows the finished bowl. Fig 5.15 shows two similar bowls which have been stained with a natural dye made from turmeric, while Fig 5.16

shows an elm platter, the centre of which has been dyed with pink silk dye, and the rim further decorated with inlays of black wood banding and brass.

FIG 5.16
An elm platter, its centre dyed with pink silk dye and surrounded with inlays of black banding and brass.

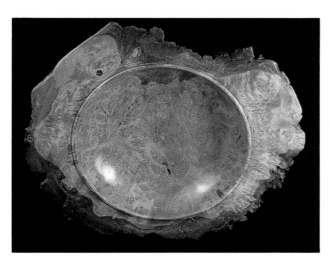

FIG 5.14
The finished bowl, with the inside coloured with blue-green water-based dye.

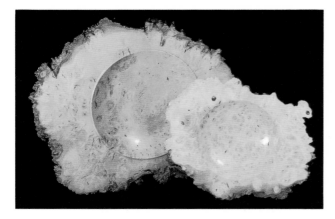

FIG 5.15
Two further oak bowls stained with turmeric-based dye.

ELM PLATTER STAINED WITH SILK DYES

This project involves a 'painting' technique using a very fine paintbrush. The starting point is an elm platter 14mm ($\frac{1}{2}$in) deep, with a diameter of 335mm (13in) and rim width 47mm ($1\frac{7}{8}$in). The bowl should be finely sanded but without any finish applied.

MATERIALS AND METHOD

Selection of water-based silk dyes

Very fine paintbrush

1 Using a very fine paintbrush, apply a variety of dilute, blended, water-based dyes carefully along selected grain bands (see Fig 5.17). Silk dyes were used in this example, but any water-based dyes could be chosen. In this way, the grain pattern can be highlighted to emphasize the wavy bands (see Fig 5.18).

2 Apply the desired finish, which in this example was sanding sealer and beeswax, both applied by hand.

Fig 5.19 shows the finished platter.

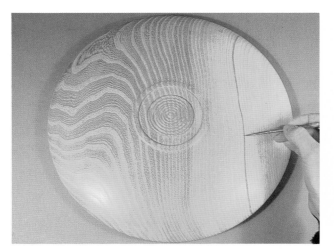

FIG 5.17
Apply dye carefully along selected grain lines, using a very fine paintbrush.

FIG 5.18
The underside of the platter, with the grain pattern highlighted by applying a range of water-based silk dyes.

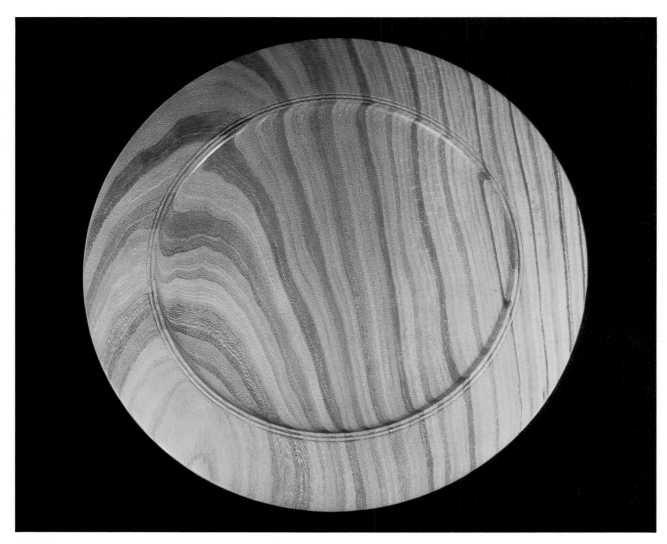

FIG 5.19
The finished platter, showing the pattern achieved on the top surface.

EBONIZED OAK BOWL

The starting point for this project is a part-turned oak bowl, attached to the lathe with a screw-chuck (see Fig 5.20). It is 96mm ($3\frac{3}{4}$in) high, with a rim diameter of 112mm ($4\frac{3}{8}$in) and a foot width of 42mm ($1\frac{5}{8}$in). The outside surface should be finely sanded but without any finish applied.

MATERIALS AND METHOD

White vinegar and iron filings solution

1 Prepare a solution of iron filings and white vinegar and leave to stand for a few days.

2 Rub the surface of the bowl with the iron and vinegar solution using a pad of wire wool (see Fig 5.21), applying several coats if necessary. Do not worry if the colour seems patchy at first – it will dry evenly.

3 Leave the surface of the wood to dry thoroughly.

4 Sand *lightly* with 0000 wire wool and burnish with a soft cloth. Apply sanding sealer followed by wax, or any other preferred finish.

5 Reverse-chuck the bowl, then turn and sand the inside.

6 Repeat steps 2–4 on the inside of the bowl.

Fig 5.22 shows the finished bowl, with decorative handles added.

FIG 5.20
Starting point: a part-turned oak bowl, attached to the lathe with a screw-chuck.

FIG 5.21
Apply iron filings and white vinegar solution to the surface of the bowl, using a pad of wire wool.

FIG 5.22
The finished ebonized bowl, complete with unusual handles.

6

WAXES AND PASTES

◆ Selection of waxes and pastes ◆ Methods of application ◆ Selection of timber ◆

PROJECTS

◆ Elm platter stained with shoe polish ◆ Elm bowl stained with black patinating wax ◆
◆ Dyed oak candlestick decorated with liming wax ◆
◆ Stained oak bangle enhanced with gilt cream ◆

ESSENTIAL EQUIPMENT

Plenty of old cloths
Wire wool
Basic turning tools and materials

RECOMMENDED EQUIPMENT

Rubber gloves
Soft wire brush

Coloured waxes, pastes and creams can be used on wood in a variety of ways to produce some unusual and striking effects. Several manufacturers now produce a range made especially for use on wood – usually for restoring furniture, although woodturners are discovering their decorative uses on turned items. Many people will be familiar with the Liberon range, while Connoisseur Studio also produce an excellent range of metallic waxes. Although these products may seem expensive at first, you will soon discover that very little is needed to complete a project, and a small pot will last a very long time.

An alternative to buying ready-made products is to make your own. Soft, colourless polishing wax, such as Briwax, can be mixed with coloured powder to produce a coloured wax. Ordinary powder paints can be used in this way, while coloured powders made specifically for mixing with waxes, varnishes and so on are available from Liberon. However, an easier and cheaper alternative is simply to use ordinary shoe polish. Indeed, it is now possible to buy such a wide range of different coloured shoe polishes that it is hardly worth making your own coloured waxes!

SELECTION OF WAXES AND PASTES

There is a huge range of products available from which to choose.

Most people are familiar with liming wax, traditionally used to lime oak. This is a soft, white wax or cream which is rubbed into the grain and left to dry, and then the surplus wiped off. The only wax which remains is that embedded in the grain. (Because the wax is white, it will often cause the overall colour of the wood to appear paler; this is particularly true if the wax is applied to dyed wood.)

Black patinating wax is very similar to liming wax except that it is black. It creates a similar effect to liming wax, but in black, and is often used to produce an 'antique' effect.

Numerous metallic waxes, creams and pastes are also available. The different shades of gold, silver and other metallic colours can look lovely if applied carefully.

METHODS OF APPLICATION

Coloured waxes and pastes can be used in a variety of ways to produce different effects. The most common method is to apply them to coarse-grained timbers to emphasize the grain patterns. Another is to use them on smooth, close-grained timbers to change the overall colour. An example of this is given in Chapter 14, where silver wax is applied on top of a black stain to create a 'pewter' effect (see page 145). This chapter focuses on the use of waxes to emphasize grain patterns.

In Chapter 5, Dyes and Stains, it was emphasized that the sanding process must be meticulous, as any tiny surface scratches will be highlighted by the dye. The same is true of coloured waxes and pastes, since they will penetrate every tiny hole, crack and pore. Care needs to be taken, therefore, to check the surface carefully for tiny defects before applying the wax – the aim is to highlight the grain pattern, not your sanding scratches!

Most coloured waxes and pastes are very dense and the colours often intense. Consequently, it is advisable to apply sanding sealer or melamine to the wood *before* applying the wax. This will ensure that the colour penetrates only the areas you want (i.e. the grain) and not the rest of the surface.

Before applying sanding sealer, many people recommend that the grain be 'opened' by brushing lightly with a soft wire brush to clean out any clogged grain pores. This is not absolutely necessary, but it can sometimes improve the finished effect. (Do make sure, though, that you use a *soft* wire brush – not the hard kind used for cleaning masonry!)

In some instances, where a more subtle effect is desired, the coloured wax or paste can be thinned before application. In many cases you can use white spirit, but check the manufacturer's instructions to see which type of thinner is recommended.

After the wax has been applied, it is left to dry and then wiped away with a soft cloth. Some finishing oil or soft, clear wax on the cloth will help to clean the surface of any surplus colour.

SELECTION OF TIMBER

If a coloured wax or paste is to be used to emphasize the grain, then clearly a coarse-grained timber must be selected. Oak, ash, elm and sweet chestnut are all good examples and can produce some beautiful results.

Waxes can be used on timber of any colour, but one would normally select a timber and a wax of contrasting colours in order to create the most striking effects. As well as using wax on the timber's natural colour, some very attractive results can be obtained by dyeing the timber first and then applying the wax.

In most of the following projects, the starting point is a part-turned item, still attached to the lathe. In fact, the procedures described can be applied to a complete item, even long after it has been turned, and need not be carried out with the item mounted on the lathe. The reason I have chosen to do so is simply because it is easier to apply wax or paste to an object which is supported on the lathe, and it is much quicker to utilize the lathe's speed for removing surplus colour and for polishing. Other that that, the following methods can be carried out on completed pieces entirely by hand and without the use of a lathe.

ELM PLATTER STAINED WITH SHOE POLISH

The starting point for this project is a half-turned elm platter 35mm (1$\frac{3}{8}$in) deep, with a diameter of 340mm (13$\frac{3}{8}$in). Fig 6.1 shows the turned underside of the platter, which is still attached to the faceplate.

MATERIALS AND METHOD

Blue and grey shoe polish

Soft, colourless polishing wax (e.g. Briwax)

1   Sand the surface of the underside of the platter finely, making sure that no sanding scratches or defects of any kind are apparent.

2   Open the grain pores by brushing lightly with a soft wire brush. Apply sanding sealer and cut back with 0000 wire wool.

FIG 6.1
Starting point: a half-turned elm platter, still attached to the faceplate.

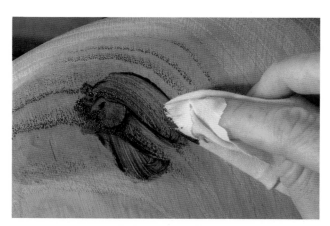

FIG 6.2
Work a mixture of grey and blue shoe polish into the grain.

3   With the lathe stationary, rub the shoe polish all over the surface using a soft cloth, ensuring that the wax is worked well into the grain pores (see Fig 6.2). In this example, a mixture of grey and blue shoe polish was used. When the entire surface has been covered, leave the wax to dry for a few minutes.

4   Put a dab of soft, colourless polishing wax on a clean, soft cloth and, with the lathe running, rub this over the surface, removing any surplus colour. The only colour then remaining should be confined to the grain pores. This buffing procedure will also serve to polish the surface nicely, so no further finishing is necessary (see Fig 6.3).

FIG 6.3
After buffing with colourless polishing wax, the only colour remaining will be confined to the grain pores.

5   Remove the platter from the lathe and reverse-chuck it to turn the inside. When the inside has been turned and sanded as before, follow steps 2–4 above.

Fig 6.4 shows the finished platter.

FIG 6.4
The completed platter, stained and finished on both surfaces.

ELM BOWL STAINED WITH BLACK PATINATING WAX

The starting point for this project is a half-turned elm bowl 15mm ($\frac{5}{8}$in) deep, with a diameter of 180mm (7in) and a rim width of 20mm ($\frac{3}{4}$in). Fig 6.5 shows the turned underside of the bowl, which is still attached to the screw-chuck.

FIG 6.5
Starting point: a half-turned elm bowl, still attached to the screw-chuck.

In this case, I chose to dye the wood before applying the wax. In fact, it is not necessary to do this, and the wax could be applied to uncoloured wood, as in the previous project.

MATERIALS AND METHOD

Selected dye (optional)

Black patinating wax

Soft, colourless polishing wax (e.g. Briwax)

1   Sand the surface of the underside of the bowl finely, making sure that no sanding scratches or defects of any kind are apparent.

2   Apply dye to the surface of the wood following the guidelines in Chapter 5 (see Fig 6.6) – this step is optional.

FIG 6.6
Apply dye to the surface of the wood, using a paintbrush.

FIG 6.7

When the dye has dried, rub black patinating wax well into the grain pores.

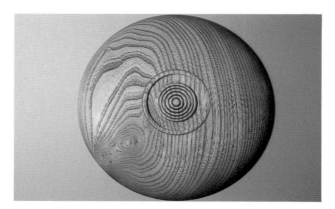

FIG 6.8

The underside, after buffing with colourless polishing wax.

3   When the dye has dried completely, brush the surface lightly with a soft wire brush to open the grain pores. Apply sanding sealer and cut back with 0000 wire wool.

4   Using a soft cloth, apply black patinating wax to the surface, rubbing it well into the grain pores (see Fig 6.7).

5   When the entire surface has been covered, leave the wax to dry for a few minutes and then, with the lathe running, wipe the surface with a small amount of soft, colourless polishing wax on a soft, clean cloth. This buffing will simultaneously remove any surplus colour and polish the surface, leaving the colour embedded in the grain (see Fig 6.8).

6   Reverse-chuck the bowl and turn the inside. Sand, and apply dye if required.

7   Repeat steps 3–5 above.

Fig 6.9 shows the finished bowl.

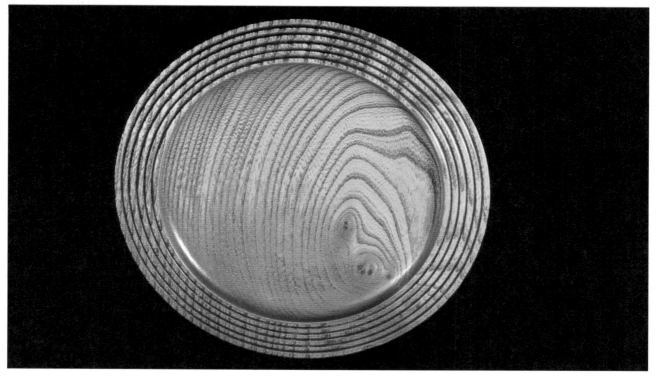

FIG 6.9

The finished bowl, with the natural grain pattern emphasized by the waxing process.

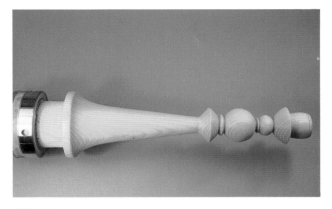

FIG 6.10
Starting point: an oak candlestick, finely sanded but still attached to the lathe.

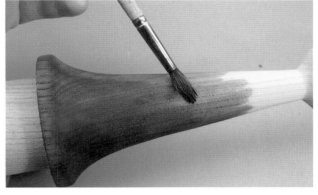

FIG 6.11
Apply water-based dye in your chosen colour, using a paintbrush.

DYED OAK CANDLESTICK DECORATED WITH LIMING WAX

The starting point for this project is a turned oak candlestick which has been sanded finely but has not been parted off from the lathe (see Fig 6.10). The candlestick is 315mm ($12\frac{3}{8}$ in) high, with a base width of 90mm ($3\frac{1}{2}$ in).

MATERIALS AND METHOD

Water-based dye

Liming wax

Soft, colourless polishing wax (e.g. Briwax)

1   Open the grain pores by brushing lightly with a soft wire brush.

2   Apply water-based dye in your chosen colour, following the guidelines in Chapter 5 (see Fig 6.11).

FIG 6.12
Rub liming wax well into the grain pores, ensuring that they are all filled.

3   Leave the dye to dry thoroughly, and then cut back *lightly* with 0000 wire wool if necessary. Apply sanding sealer.

4   With the lathe stationary, use a soft cloth to rub white liming wax into the grain pores, making sure that they are all filled (see Fig 6.12). Leave to dry for a few minutes.

5   With the lathe running, remove excess wax using a small amount of soft, colourless polishing wax on a cloth and buffing to a shine. The only liming wax remaining should be that which is firmly embedded in the grain.

6   Part off the candlestick from the lathe and finish the underside of the base, following steps 1–5 by hand.

> ## TIP
> The wood does not necessarily have to be dyed before applying the wax, but if you are using a pale wood it is advisable to dye it a darker colour, since liming wax looks best against a darker wood for maximum contrast.

Fig 6.13 shows the finished candlestick. A ring of polished pewter has been added to the inside of the candle holder for extra effect.

FIG 6.13
The finished candlestick, complete with polished pewter trim.

STAINED OAK BANGLE ENHANCED WITH GILT CREAM

The starting point for this project is a finely sanded oak bangle 40mm ($1\frac{5}{8}$in) wide, with an internal diameter of 67mm ($2\frac{5}{8}$in) and an external diameter of 88mm ($3\frac{1}{2}$in) (see Fig 6.14).

MATERIALS AND METHOD

White vinegar and iron filings solution

Gold cream

Soft, colourless polishing wax (e.g. Briwax)

1 Remount the bangle on the lathe using (preferably) a 65mm ($2\frac{1}{2}$in) expanding dovetail collet (see Fig 6.15).

FIG 6.14
Starting point: a simple oak bangle, ready for staining.

FIG 6.15
An expanding dovetail collet.

FIG 6.16
Stain the wood using a solution of iron filings and white vinegar.

FIG 6.18
The finished bangle, showing a good contrast between the dark, stained oak and the gilt cream.

FIG 6.17
Rub gilt cream into the grain pores, using a soft cloth.

FIG 6.19
A similar bangle, using copper paste instead of gilt cream.

2   With the lathe stationary, stain the bangle black by applying a solution of iron filings and vinegar – see Chapter 5 for details (see Fig 6.16).

3   When the bangle has dried thoroughly, apply sanding sealer. Then, using a soft cloth, rub gilt cream into the grain pores and leave to dry for a few minutes (see Fig 6.17).

4   With the lathe running, remove the excess wax using a small amount of soft, colourless polishing wax on a soft cloth, and buff to a shine.

Fig 6.18 shows the finished bangle. The gilt cream contrasts well with the black colour of the stained oak. Fig 6.19 shows a similar bangle where copper paste has been used instead of gilt cream.

7

INKS AND PAINTS

◆ Inks ◆ Paints ◆ Methods of application ◆ Finishes ◆

PROJECTS

◆ Indian ink on a bowl rim ◆ Spray paint on a sycamore vase ◆

ESSENTIAL EQUIPMENT

Assorted paintbrushes and pens
Basic turning tools and materials

RECOMMENDED EQUIPMENT

Plenty of newspapers and rags
Solvents and thinners
Rubber gloves

Because there is such a wide range of different types of paints and inks available, it is very difficult to generalize about their properties and effects. As always, different products will give different results, these depending largely upon the colour and opacity of the paint or ink in question.

INKS

Inks are available in a huge range of different colours. Most tend to be semi-transparent and *can* be used for colouring wood, but many brands are not very lightfast, so this is something which would need to be checked beforehand. If wood is to be coloured, there is perhaps little reason for using ink as opposed to a standard dye – dyes are generally more lightfast and cheaper. However, there are times when inks are preferable. Metallic inks, for example, can be very useful, as they can be applied in fine lines with a pen. These inks are readily available from art and craft shops, and Chapter 8 deals with them in more detail.

Indian ink can be very useful where a rich, deep black is required, as this can be hard to obtain with standard dyes. Indian ink is available from art shops in a waterproof or non-waterproof form, and before you apply it to wood you will need to check which finishes are compatible with the type of ink you have chosen. Unlike dye, Indian ink comes in small bottles, so it is not economical to use it on very large areas. It is ideal, though, for use on the rim or foot of a vase or bowl as a 'trim'.

PAINTS

As already mentioned, paints are opaque and will therefore conceal the wood grain. Consequently, you need to consider very carefully the reasons for using paint, and the desired effect. Like Indian ink, paint can be used effectively to highlight localized areas. If the entire object is to be painted, however, it must be appreciated that the item may no longer be identifiable as wood. It is for this reason that many turners will not consider applying paint to turned items. Nevertheless, there are others who feel that, in certain circumstances, it does not

matter that the finished item does not appear to be 'wooden': the important factor may be that the completed piece has grace and elegance and is pleasing to the eye, and its constitution is therefore irrelevant.

In the end, it is all a matter of personal preference. Personally, I tend not to use paint of any colour except black. I cannot *defend* this preference, but I can *explain* it by saying that, in my opinion, certain items can be particularly attractive (to me) when sprayed with a matt or semi-matt black, and the effect is one which can enhance the graceful line and form of, say, a vase, since there are no changes of colour or grain pattern to distract from the pure shape. Ultimately, there are no 'rules', of course, and the turner is at liberty to select, reject or adapt, according to personal taste.

METHODS OF APPLICATION

Inks are normally applied with a pen or fine brush. Paints can be applied with a brush, or can be sprayed on to the wood. It is advisable to practise applying any paint or ink to a piece of scrap wood first, since it is not always as easy as it might appear. Occasionally, brushmarks or streaks may appear, although this tends to happen only if relatively large areas are being covered. It can sometimes be avoided by thinning with a suitable solvent, but if streaks continue to appear with a particular ink or paint try switching to a different brand.

SPRAY PAINTS

Spray paints can be very useful for covering large areas evenly. I tend to use a matt or semi-matt black spray paint manufactured for use on cars. Remember, though, that despite the opacity of the paint, and the fact that several layers will be applied, surface defects or blemishes will *not* be hidden. If anything, they will be *emphasized*, so once again, surface quality needs to be checked carefully.

When using spray paint, do not be tempted to spray too closely to the item in question or too heavily, as this will result in surplus paint running down the sides and you will have to waste time rubbing it off when it is dry. It is quicker and simpler in the long run to be patient and spray a little bit a time, leave it to dry, and then spray another bit.

FINISHES

Once again, it is impossible to generalize because of the wide range of paints and inks available, which will vary in their compatability with various finishes. This will depend on the base from which the paint or ink has been prepared. As with dyes, a water-based product will tend to be the most versatile, being compatible with most finishes. An oil-based product will be incompatible with an oil-based finish, and a spirit-based finish cannot usually be used over a spirit-based ink or paint. Unfortunately, it is not always possible to discover the base of any given product, so you will need to test for compatibility beforehand on pieces of scrap wood. Should you have difficulty in finding a compatible finish, spray-on melamine will usually work if all else fails.

INDIAN INK ON A BOWL RIM

The starting point for this project is a spalted beech bowl 40mm ($1\frac{5}{8}$ in) deep, with a diameter of 180mm (7in) and a rim width of 8mm ($\frac{5}{16}$ in) (see Fig 7.1). It is attached to the lathe for ease of handling only. The bowl has been finely sanded but no finish has been applied.

FIG 7.1

Starting point: a spalted beech bowl, attached to the lathe for ease of handling.

MATERIALS AND METHOD

Indian ink

1   Using a fine paintbrush, carefully paint Indian ink on to the bowl rim as shown in Fig 7.2. A steady hand is required, and care must be taken not to spill over on to the rest of the bowl. This is helped to a certain extent by the groove that delineates the rim from the surrounding area. If any paint does go beyond the boundary, it can usually be sanded away when dry. (In this example, a tiny smudge on the spalted beech would probably not have been noticeable anyway, being camouflaged by the black patterning of the spalt!)

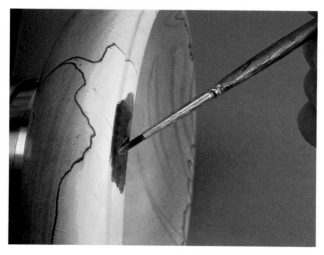

FIG 7.2

Carefully paint Indian ink on to the rim of the bowl, using a fine paintbrush.

2   When the painting is complete, there is no need to re-sand. Simply burnish with a soft cloth and apply a finish which is compatible with the type of ink used.

Fig 7.3 shows the finished bowl. Spalted beech is particularly suitable for this technique, as the black trim tends to enhance the black spalt pattern. Fig 7.4 shows a vase with Indian ink applied to the rim and foot.

FIG 7.3
The black ink trim enhances the spalt pattern of the finished bowl.

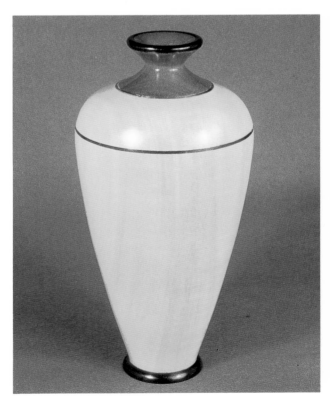

FIG 7.4
An elegant vase, with Indian ink trim on the rim and foot.

SPRAY PAINT ON A SYCAMORE VASE

The starting point for this project is a sycamore vase 165mm ($6\frac{1}{2}$in) high, with a shoulder width of 95mm ($3\frac{3}{4}$in) and a foot width of 40mm ($1\frac{5}{8}$in) (see Fig 7.5). The vase has been finely sanded but no finish has been applied.

MATERIALS AND METHOD

Semi-matt spray paint

1   Place the vase upright in a cardboard box and spray *gently* with a semi-matt spray paint (see Fig 7.6). Hold the paint can at least 30cm

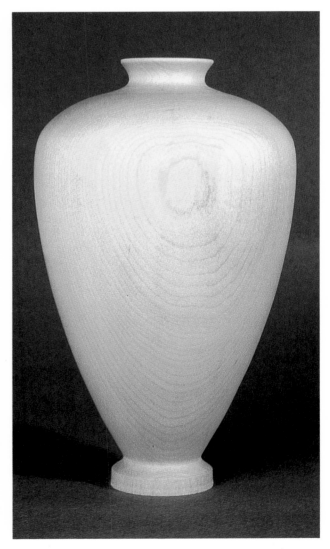

FIG 7.5
Starting point: a finely sanded sycamore vase.

71

(12in) away from the vase and keep it moving. In this example, an ordinary aerosol can of acrylic-based car-body spray paint was used. It requires no further finish on top, as it dries to a dull sheen and is quite durable.

2 When one area has been sprayed, leave it to dry, turn the vase slightly, and spray the next area. Eventually, the entire vase will be a uniform black. (Do not forget to paint the underside of the base.)

Fig 7.7 shows the finished vase.

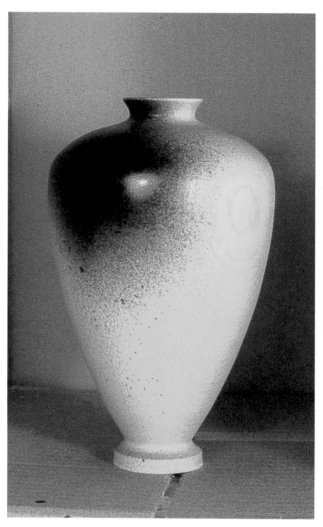

FIG 7.6
Spray the vase one section at a time, using a spray box to minimize mess.

FIG 7.7
The finished vase – a uniform semi-matt black.

8
GILDING

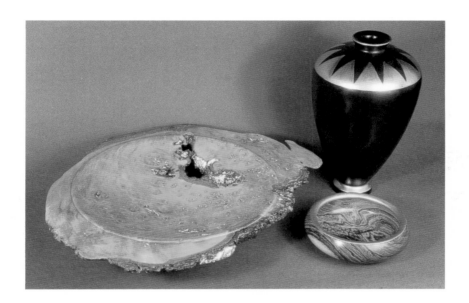

◆ Paints and varnishes ◆ Inks ◆ Powders ◆ Finishes ◆

PROJECTS

◆ Gilt varnish on a bowl rim ◆ Gold powder on a burr oak bowl ◆
◆ Gold paint and ink on a black-sprayed vase ◆

ESSENTIAL EQUIPMENT

Several fine paintbrushes
Thinners (if necessary)
Basic turning tools and materials

Traditionally, gilding was done by trained craftsmen, using gold leaf. Gold leaf is still used today in some crafts, and both gold and silver leaf can be purchased through mail order. However, the technique is extremely difficult and requires many hours of practice, not to mention patience. Even then, it can be difficult to get a smooth, even surface. For these reasons, this chapter explores a variety of easier methods, using a wide range of different gilding products including powders, paints, varnishes and inks. Metallic waxes can also be used for gilding, following the guidelines in Chapter 6.

Gilding is best done on small, localized areas, using the gilding substance sparingly to add a subtle highlight. Used in this way, gilding is far more successful than when an item is over-gilded. The three basic techniques used for the projects in this chapter can be adapted to enhance any woodturned item.

PAINTS AND VARNISHES

Metallic paints are readily available from art and craft shops and there is a wide range from which to choose. Gold, silver and copper are the most common colours, and within the gold range alone it is possible to select from many different 'shades'. Connoisseur Studio produce an excellent range of good-quality metallic paints, while Liberon also produce a range of gilt varnishes, which require no further finish after application.

All metallic paints need to be shaken thoroughly before (and in some cases during) use, since the tiny gilt particles tend to sink to the bottom of the bottle very rapidly. Apply them to the surface with a brush, in the usual way. Avoid 'over-brushing', since this can result in streaks. If this does occur, you may find it helpful to thin the paint using a proprietary thinner.

INKS

Metallic inks can be purchased in bottles or in the form of ink pens. Felt-tip pens in gold and silver are very useful for producing fine, accurate lines, and give a good metallic finish. Choose a wide, medium or fine tip, depending on the area to be covered.

POWDERS

Gold and silver powders, available from art shops, are produced by a number of different manufacturers, and the different products vary according to the 'mesh', or 'fineness', of the particles. Generally speaking, the finer the particles, the better the finished effect, so it is worth shopping around for the best products. With extremely fine particles, you get a really good gold or silver, whereas with coarser particles, the silver powder tends to give a greyer effect and the gold just looks yellow.

Metallic powders are quite versatile; they can be mixed with clear lacquer and applied as a varnish, or mixed with clear wax and applied as a paste. The powder can also be rubbed into cracks and crevices in the wood to produce a jewel-like effect.

FINISHES

The type of finish will, once again, depend on the type of gilding product used. As always, experiment on scrap wood first to check which finishes are compatible with your chosen gilding product. Some products, such as varnishes, do not require a finish on top, but this depends on the amount of handling the item is likely to receive day to day. After a while you will become familiar with the types of finish compatible with various commercial products. Very often the manufacturers state which finish can be applied, and/or produce their own range of finishes.

GILT VARNISH ON A BOWL RIM

The starting point for this project is a bocote bowl 28mm ($1\frac{1}{8}$in) deep, with a diameter of 90mm ($3\frac{1}{2}$in). The rim, measuring 6mm ($\frac{1}{4}$in), is undercut on the inside. The bowl is sanded and finished with sanding sealer and carnauba wax, although no finish has been applied to the rim (see Fig 8.1).

MATERIALS AND METHOD

Fontenay base

Gilt varnish

1   Paint a thin layer of Fontenay base on to the rim of the bowl (see Fig 8.2). This acts as a sealer and provides an 'undertone' to the gilt. When the Fontenay base is dry, sand the area lightly.

2   Using a fine paintbrush, carefully paint the bowl rim using gilt varnish (see Fig 8.3). In this example, a fine groove has been cut around the edge of the rim to delineate it from the surrounding area, and this helps to prevent overspill of the varnish.

3   When the varnish has dried, check the surface carefully – it may need a second coat. When you are satisfied with the results, no further finish is necessary.

Fig 8.4 shows the finished bowl.

FIG 8.1
Starting point: a bocote bowl, the rim of which is unfinished, ready for gilding.

FIG 8.3
Paint over the Fontenay base with gilt varnish, using a fine paintbrush.

FIG 8.2
Paint a thin layer of Fontenay base on to the rim of the bowl.

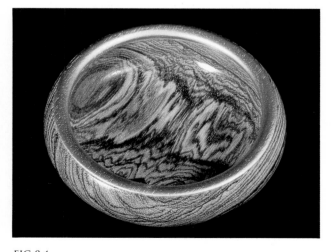

FIG 8.4
The finished bowl, with gilded rim.

GOLD POWDER ON A BURR OAK BOWL

The starting point for this project is a burr oak bowl with a maximum width of 255mm (10in) and depth of 35mm (1⅜in). It has been sanded and

FIG 8.5

Starting point: two views of the burr oak bowl, chosen for its natural crevices – ideal for filling with gold powder.

finished with melamine. The melamine has then been cut back with fine wire wool to give a soft sheen (see Fig 8.5).

Burr oak was chosen for this project because of the natural crevices in the surface into which the gold powder could be applied. The inspiration came from observing various mineral ores, in particular iron pyrites. I wished to reproduce the effect of tiny deposits of 'gold' within the surrounding medium.

MATERIALS AND METHOD

Melamine

Gold powder

1   Look carefully at the bowl and decide which cracks and crevices you wish to decorate with the gold powder. You will probably not want to do all of them – aim for a 'balanced' look.

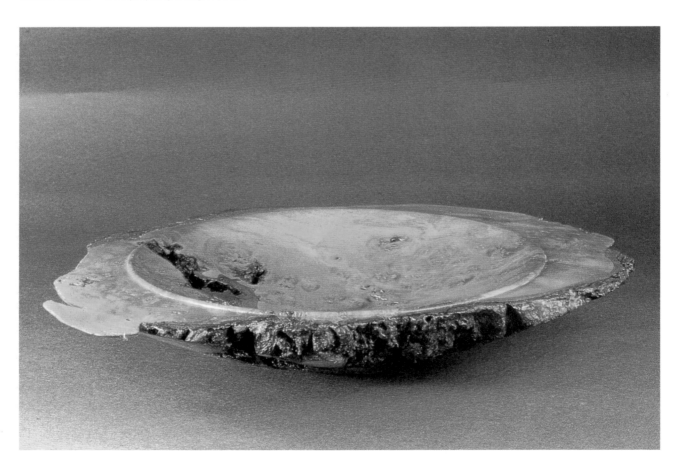

2   Starting with one of your chosen crevices, apply a small amount of melamine to the area with a fine paintbrush (see Fig 8.6).

3   Before the melamine has had time to dry, brush some gold powder over the same area using a different, and slightly thicker brush (it is important to keep the two brushes separate). The gold powder will adhere readily to the sticky melamine, and as the melamine dries, the powder will be bonded securely to the wood within the crevice. Work on just a small area at a time: if you try to do too much at once, the melamine will have dried before you have had time to apply the powder.

4   Repeat with the next crack or crevice, until all the selected areas have been gilded. This can be done on both sides of the bowl, or one side only. In this example, both sides are gilded. No further finish is necessary.

Fig 8.7 shows the completed bowl.

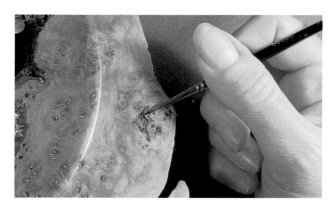

FIG 8.6
Apply melamine to the selected crevices, using a fine paintbrush.

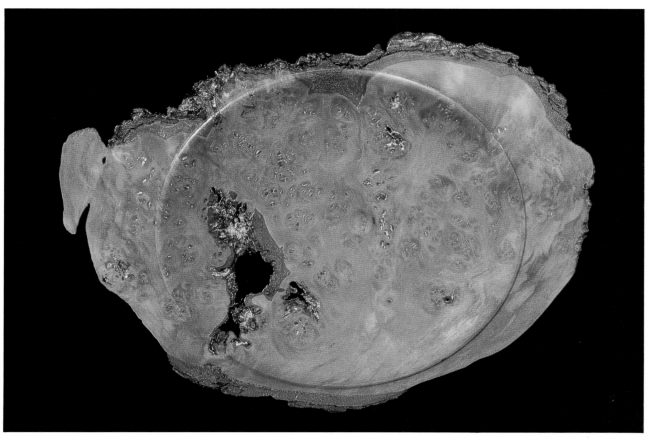

FIG 8.7
The finished bowl, with tiny 'gold' deposits nestling in its crevices.

GOLD PAINT AND INK ON A BLACK-SPRAYED VASE

The starting point for this project is the black-sprayed sycamore vase in Chapter 7 (see Fig 7.7 on page 72).

MATERIALS AND METHOD

Fine-point gold ink pen

Gold paint

1 For ease of handling, remount the vase on the lathe as shown in Fig 8.8. A recess has been cut into a piece of scrap wood on the headstock, into which the base of the vase is inserted. The

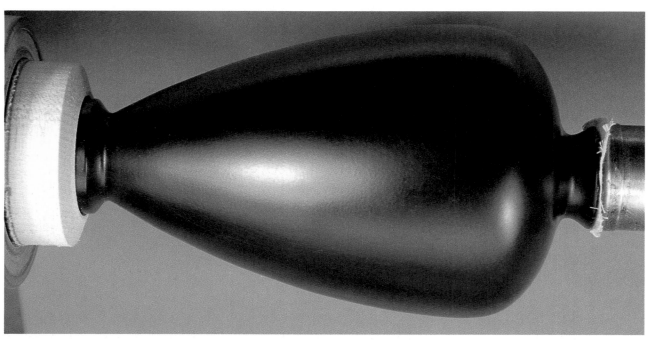

FIG 8.8
Remount the vase on the lathe for ease of handling.

FIG 8.9
Draw in the outlines of the area to be painted, using a fine-point gold pen.

tailstock is then brought up to support the neck of the vase, with some protective cloth placed between the tailstock and the vase neck. This device holds the vase securely while allowing it to be rotated slowly by hand. This method is not obligatory, but it does make the painting easier.

2 Decide on your design, and mark out the boundaries of the pattern in pencil.

3 Using a fine-point gold ink pen, carefully draw in the outline of the areas to be painted to give a clear, defined edge (see Fig 8.9).

4 Block in the areas within the boundaries with gold paint.

5 Using the gold ink pen, apply a fine line around the rim of the vase and a broader line just above the base.

Fig 8.10 shows the finished vase. If it is not likely to receive a great deal of handling, there is no need to apply a further finish. You may, however, wish to add a protective sealing layer if greater durability is required.

FIG 8.10
The finished vase, with the gold pattern blocked in and gold trim added at the rim and base.

PART THREE

WOOD-COMPOSITE
TECHNIQUES

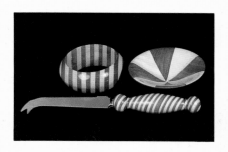

Laminating and the use of Veneers

Stickwork

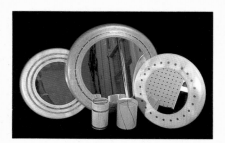

Inlaying Wood Bandings and Plugs

INTRODUCTION

The term 'wood-composite techniques' refers to the assembly of many different-coloured pieces of timber to form a combined whole. The composite block thus formed can then be turned on the lathe in the same way as an ordinary blank.

There are many ways in which different timbers can be combined. This section focuses on just some of them: laminating and the use of veneers, stickwork, and the inlaying of wood bandings and plugs. The techniques described are all very straightforward, and simple projects have been selected. However, for those who like a challenge, very much more complex methods of segmented work are possible, by slowly building up large pieces from elaborately cut small pieces of wood, and some beautifully intricate work can be produced in this way.

LAMINATING

Laminating involves cutting layers of different-coloured timbers and then gluing them one upon the other, to produce a striped effect. The exact visual effect depends upon the width of the laminates, the variety of timbers used, and the way in which they have been assembled.

VENEERS

Veneers are very thin sheets of timber usually produced for use in cabinet making and marquetry. They can, however, be glued between larger pieces of wood and turned, creating the effect of thin lines or bands of a different colour running through the length of the work.

STICKWORK

In stickwork, small rods of different-coloured woods are glued in a random or regular fashion, to form a composite block consisting of many different colours. The visual pattern created in this way depends upon the shape of the cross-section of the rods and the arrangement of the colours in relation to each other.

WOOD BANDINGS

These are thin strips of ready-prepared veneer made up from tiny segments of different-coloured wood arranged in a regular pattern. They can be used for inlaying into turned items and will produce a variety of effects, according to the method of inlay. Bandings are useful for decorating items such as boxes, goblets and small bowls. They are inlaid simply by cutting a goove to the correct size and gluing the strips in place.

WOODEN PLUGS

These are small cylinders of wood which can be cut easily from any scrap of wood using a plug cutter. The plugs can be inlaid into the surface of any piece of wood by drilling holes of the appropriate size and gluing the plugs in place.

SELECTION OF TIMBER

Dense, close-grained timbers in a variety of different colours are ideal for these methods. Try to choose colours which contrast well, and think carefully about how the colours should be arranged: do you want a random effect, or are you aiming for a regular pattern with the colours arranged in a certain order?

Small offcuts can often be used in some of these techniques, and this is a good way of using up leftover pieces which might otherwise be thrown away. It is a good idea, therefore, to keep a box of these offcuts ready for later use.

PRECISION

Many of the techniques outlined in this section call for a high degree of precision, especially where cutting and assembly is concerned. Without this, the pieces will not fit together as they should, so it is worth taking time over the preparatory stages.

ADHESIVES

Any strong woodworking adhesive can be used. It is always a good idea to use a brand which has given you good results before, although in recent years many new products have been produced that are worth trying.

PVA glue is fine for the techniques described in this section, although it does have a tendency to allow the layers to 'creep' slightly over the months following assembly, necessitating further sanding at a later date. Cascamite does not do this and appears to be relatively stable over time.

EQUIPMENT

The equipment required will vary according to the type of composite work being undertaken. In some instances, very little special equipment is required. In others, such as diamond stickwork, precise cutting machinery is required. *It is inadvisable to attempt methods which require the use of such machinery unless you have some previous experience in its use.*

9
LAMINATING AND THE USE OF VENEERS

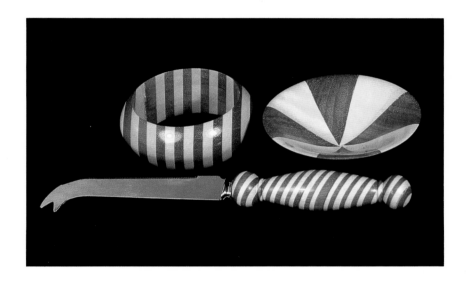

◆ Selection of timber ◆ Laminating with wood cut on the bandsaw ◆ Using veneers ◆

PROJECTS

◆ Laminated knife handle ◆ Small 'coopered' bowl ◆
◆ Sycamore and padauk veneered vase ◆ Small veneered box ◆ Veneered padauk bowl ◆

ESSENTIAL EQUIPMENT

Bandsaw
Strong wood adhesive
Assorted clamps
Basic turning tools and materials

RECOMMENDED EQUIPMENT

Planer-thicknesser

Sheets, or 'laminates', of different woods can be glued together to form a composite block for turning on the lathe. By choosing timbers of contrasting colours, a variety of attractive striped patterns can be produced. The first part of this chapter explores the laminating of thin layers of different-coloured woods which have been cut on a bandsaw. The second part demonstrates the use of veneers to produce similar, but rather different, effects.

SELECTION OF TIMBER

Generally speaking, it is best to choose fine-grained rather than coarse-grained timbers. Try also to select plain timbers, avoiding those which have a pronounced figure. Timbers which are already striped, such as zebrano, or which have contrasting colours of heartwood and sapwood in the same piece, should be avoided.

Timbers which have a good, strong, consistent colour throughout are ideal. Choose colours which will contrast well, since this will increase the visual impact of the stripes. Good examples are sycamore, lime, purpleheart, padauk, holly, amarello and dark rosewoods.

COLOUR COMBINATIONS

The actual colour combinations you choose are entirely a matter of personal taste and availability of timbers. Always combine dark and light colours if possible; for example, sycamore and purpleheart will provide a better contrast than, say sycamore and lime.

Any number of colour combinations can be used in one piece making laminating one of the techniques that is good for using up unwanted offcuts. For the sake of simplicity, however, the techniques described below refer to the use of two contrasting timbers only.

LAMINATING WITH WOOD CUT ON THE BANDSAW

PLANNING

There are a number of aesthetic considerations to take into account before commencing work. A wide variety of different visual effects can be produced, so it is worth deciding at the start which particular effect to aim for.

LAMINATE THICKNESS

The laminates can be cut to any thickness, depending on personal taste and the effect desired. It is wise to use thin laminates for small items, but bear in mind that the thinner the laminates, the more you will have to prepare and glue, thus increasing the time and labour involved. To begin with, then, you may prefer to use laminates which are relatively thick.

It is usual to keep all the laminates the same thickness, although different thicknesses can be combined successfully (see Fig 9.1).

STRIPE DIRECTION

There are a number of ways in which laminates can be assembled into a composite block to produce different effects.

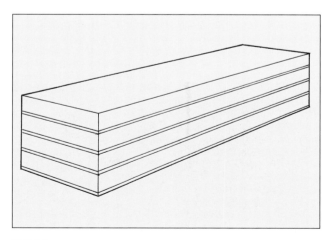

FIG 9.1
Laminates can be of different thicknesses.

Longitudinal stripes Here the laminates are assembled so that the stripes run in the same direction as the axis of the block. If the block is to be used for spindle turning, this means that the stripes will run parallel to the lathe bed (see Fig 9.2). If preparing a circular blank for faceplate turning, the direction of the stripes is as shown in Fig 9.3.

Lateral stripes In this case, the stripes run perpendicular to the axis of the block (see Fig 9.4). This is less suitable for spindle turning than longitudinal stripes, because the direction of the grain is inconsistent. The assembly for faceplate turning is shown in Fig 9.5. Fig 9.6 shows a bangle which has been turned from a block with lateral stripes.

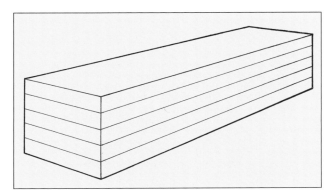

FIG 9.2
Longitudinal stripes (spindle turning).

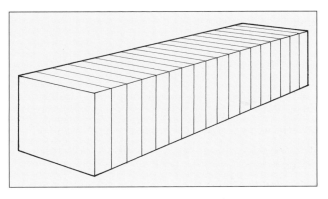

FIG 9.4
Lateral stripes (spindle turning).

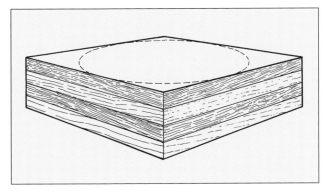

FIG 9.3
Longitudinal stripes (faceplate turning).

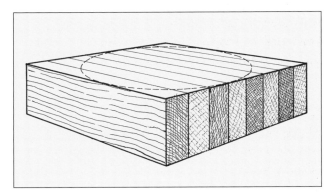

FIG 9.5
Lateral stripes (faceplate turning).

FIG 9.6
A bangle turned from a block with lateral stripes.

Diagonal stripes Here the stripes run diagonally across the axis of the composite block, as shown in Fig 9.7.

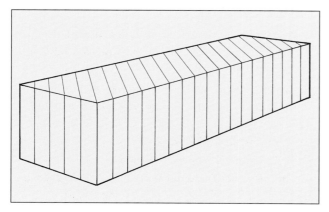

FIG 9.7
Diagonal stripes (spindle turning).

PREPARATION OF THE LAMINATES

The first step is to cut the laminates. The size of the blocks from which they are to be cut, and the direction of the cut, will depend on the overall dimensions required for the finished composite block and the direction intended for the stripes.

For longitudinal laminates, the cut will very often be parallel with the grain of the original blocks (see Fig 9.8). This is where a sharp bandsaw

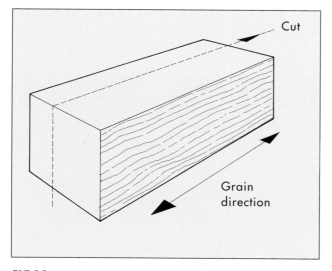

FIG 9.8
When cutting longitudinal laminates from a rectangular block, the cuts will be parallel to the grain direction.

blade is absolutely essential, otherwise it will tend to 'wander' off course.

For lateral laminates, the cut may be either parallel or perpendicular to the grain. (The terms longitudinal and lateral as used here refer not to the grain orientation but to the direction of the stripes relative to the composite block.)

Diagonal laminates are cut by removing the 'corner' and presenting the original block at an angle to the blade (see Fig 9.9).

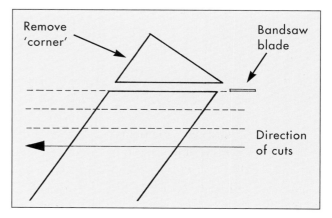

FIG 9.9
To cut diagonal laminates, present the block at an angle to the bandsaw blade and remove the 'corner'.

For best results, follow the guidelines below.

- The laminates should all be the same thickness. As already mentioned, the thickness can be varied deliberately to produce a specific effect. However, if it is your *intention* to produce laminates of the same thickness, it does look better if they actually *are*! Having decided upon the desired thickness, set up the bandsaw with the rip fence in the appropriate position, and cut all the laminates in one go if possible. This will ensure consistency. If you have access to a planer-thicknesser, this is even better, and it can be used to thickness the laminates to the precise dimensions.

- The surfaces to be bonded should be absolutely flat. If two adjacent surfaces are rough or uneven, this will result in gaps that will look unsightly when the block is turned. It is important, therefore, to ensure that all surfaces are as flat as possible. This can be achieved by some form of mechanical sanding (such as an orbital or disc sander), or better still by using a planer if one is available. When cutting the laminates on the bandsaw, always use a very sharp blade. This will make cutting easier and will also give a smoother cut.

- The direction of the grain should be consistent. When assembling the laminates, make sure that the grain direction matches. Not only does this look better, but it will make turning much easier.

ASSEMBLY

When all the laminates have been prepared, place them together in order, checking to see that they fit and that the effect is what you had intended. When you are satisfied, glue them together in stages. Do not attempt to glue them all up at once, because it is likely that they will slide out of alignment while the glue is drying. It is better to glue up a few at a time, perhaps in pairs or threes, and then, when the glue has dried, glue up these smaller piles into larger blocks. Make sure, too, that the pieces are clamped securely, but do not over-tighten the clamps.

Once the laminate blocks have dried, they can be trimmed if necessary on the bandsaw prior to turning.

COOPERING

Coopering is the name given to the traditional craft of barrel making, which required a high degree of precision and skill. Nowadays, the term has (somewhat incorrectly, perhaps) been broadened to apply to any method of assembling different pieces of wood in a radial fashion, and I use it here to describe the radial assembly of wooden segments to form a circle.

The number of segments used is, once again, a matter of personal taste. Fig 9.10 shows two possible configurations, one using eight segments, the other ten. Any number can be used, but the angles of cut must be worked out carefully to ensure a good fit. In this respect, an eight-segment construction is perhaps the easiest, because it can be assembled from two circles of wood of contrasting colours, each circle being cut into eight equal segments (see Fig 9.11). The small bowl on page 90 has been 'coopered' using this method, gluing the segments together and clamping the complete circle with a large jubilee clip.

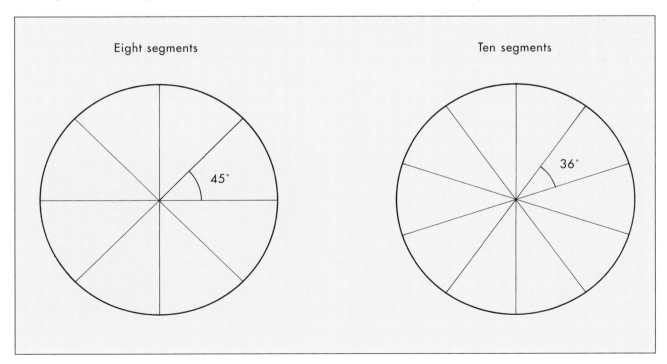

FIG 9.10
Two options for assembling wooden segments to form a circle.

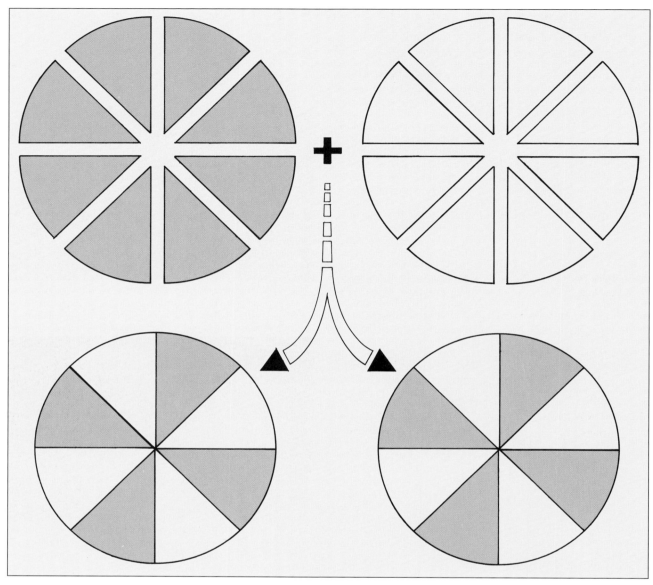

FIG 9.11
An eight-segment configuration can be assembled from two circles of wood in contrasting colours.

LAMINATED KNIFE HANDLE

The starting point for this project is a composite block of diagonal laminates made from sycamore and purpleheart. The block is 120mm ($4\frac{3}{4}$in) long, with a cross-section 35mm ($1\frac{3}{8}$in) square (see Fig 9.12). In this example, not all the laminates are exactly the same thickness. The reason for this is that the block was made from a collection of offcuts from previous laminates, which were not all the same size, but were too small to be sawed or planed further. Not wishing to waste the wood,

FIG 9.12
Starting point: a block of diagonal sycamore and purpleheart laminates.

I made up a composite blank from these offcuts. The minor discrepancies in thickness detract slightly from the overall effect, but this can be offset against the satisfaction of having salvaged the material which would otherwise have been in the wastebin, and the knowledge that the finished handle, in effect, cost nothing except time.

MATERIALS AND METHOD

Superglue (optional)

Knife tang

1   Glue the composite block to a wooden faceplate using superglue. (This method of chucking was chosen for its ease and speed and to minimize wastage, but other methods would also be suitable.) Rough down the blank to a cylinder.

2   Insert a drill chuck into the tailstock and attach a drill bit of the appropriate size for the knife tang. In this example, a 6mm ($\frac{1}{4}$in) drill bit was used. With the lathe running at its slowest speed, drill into the end of the blank to a depth corresponding to the length of the knife tang (see Fig 9.13).

3   Replace the drill chuck with a revolving tailstock and bring this up to support the end of the blank. Begin to shape the handle.

4   When a satisfactory shape has been achieved, sand and apply a hardwearing, water- and heat-proof finish (see Fig 9.14).

5   Part off, and finish the end of the handle by hand.

Fig 9.15 shows the finished knife, with the blade inserted and glued in place.

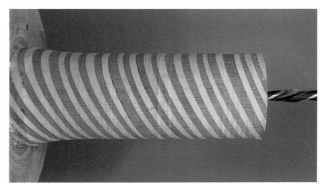

FIG 9.13
Drill a hole into the end of the cylinder to take the knife tang.

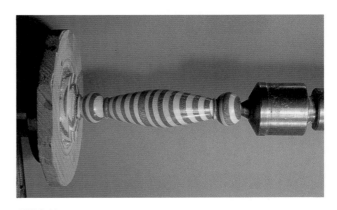

FIG 9.14
The turned handle, sanded and finished.

FIG 9.15
The finished knife, with the laminates giving almost a spiral effect.

SMALL 'COOPERED' BOWL

The starting point for this project is two circular bowl blanks in contrasting woods. In this example, sycamore and purpleheart were used. Each bowl blank was cut into eight equal segments and reassembled to form two new composite blanks, as already shown in Fig 9.11. One of these blanks, 100mm (4in) in diameter and 50mm (2in) deep, was used for this project (see Fig 9.16).

METHOD

1 Attach the composite blank to the lathe by means of a screw-chuck, and rough down to a cylinder.

2 Turn the outside of the bowl, including a small foot for insertion into a contracting collet chuck. (Alternative means of reverse-chucking would be equally acceptable, but would alter the design slightly.) Sand and finish (see Fig 9.17).

3 Reverse-chuck the bowl and turn the inside. Sand and finish.

   Fig 9.18 shows the finished bowl.

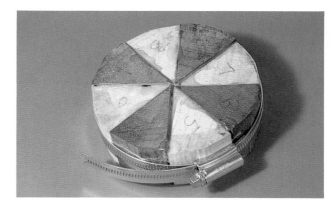

FIG 9.16
A 'coopered' blank, clamped with a large jubilee clip.

FIG 9.17
The underside of the bowl, turned and finished.

FIG 9.18
The finished bowl, showing the pattern of the laminates inside and out.

USING VENEERS

As we have seen, the preparation of laminates can be time consuming. It also requires the use of cutting machinery. For those who wish to use a simpler method which avoids the initial preparatory phases, the use of veneers may provide a satisfactory alternative. Of course, the visual effects are somewhat different, but certainly no less pleasing. Indeed, you may prefer the more subtle effects created by the thin, elegant lines of veneer.

SELECTION OF VENEERS

Veneers are available in a wide variety of different woods, and accordingly the prices vary enormously. When choosing veneer, it is important to remember that the majority of woodworkers use it for the subtle and attractive grain patterns to be found on its surface: in cabinet-making, marquetry and other forms of inlay work, the grain pattern is all-important. The same is not true for the techniques described here, since the surface of the veneer is not exposed, and only the narrow sides will be visible. So, for these purposes, colour – not attractive grain pattern – is the main criterion. There would be no point in buying a sheet of expensive birdseye maple, for example, since ordinary plain maple or sycamore, which is much cheaper, would do the same job.

The price of veneer also varies according to the supplier. It is worth shopping around, because some retailers charge very high prices for relatively small pieces, whereas others sell it in larger sheets for half the price.

Always handle veneers carefully. Being very thin, they break exceptionally easily, so store them safely out of harm's way.

ASSEMBLY

The procedures for gluing up are the same as for laminates. Use a good, strong wood glue, and clamp the pieces securely until dry.

SYCAMORE AND PADAUK VENEERED VASE

The starting point for this project is made up of two distinct elements. First, for the vase body you will need a block of sycamore 310mm ($12\frac{3}{16}$in) long, with a cross-section 120mm ($4\frac{3}{4}$in) square, plus two pieces of padauk veneer each 120mm ($4\frac{3}{4}$in) wide but only 260mm ($10\frac{3}{16}$in) long (see Fig 9.19). The veneer does not need to be quite as long as the sycamore block because some of the latter will be wasted in the chuck and in parting off. Second, for the vase neck you will need a block of padauk 160mm ($6\frac{1}{4}$in) long, with a cross-section 75mm (3in) square, plus two pieces of sycamore veneer each 160mm ($6\frac{1}{4}$in) long and 75mm (3in) wide (see Fig 9.20).

FIG 9.19
Starting point 1: a sycamore block and padauk veneers.

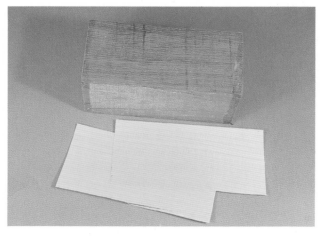

FIG 9.20
Starting point 2: a padauk block and sycamore veneers.

MATERIALS AND METHOD

Superglue

1 Using a bandsaw, cut the sycamore block in half lengthways. Glue the two halves back together, with one of the padauk veneers sandwiched in between. Clamp and leave to dry.

2 Cut the block in half lengthways again but in the other plane. As before, glue the two halves back together, with the second padauk veneer in between (see Fig 9.21). Clamp and leave to dry.

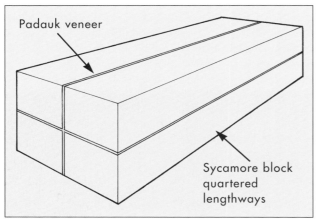

FIG 9.21
Glue the quartered sycamore block back together, sandwiching the padauk veneer in between.

3 Repeat steps 1 and 2 with the padauk block and sycamore veneers (see Fig 9.22).

4 When the glue has dried, mount the sycamore composite block between centres and rough down to a cylinder. Reverse-chuck so that the blank is firmly supported at the headstock end only (in this example a 3-way split pin method was used, but any preferred method could be employed). Make sure that the end without the veneer in it is at the headstock end, since this is where the waste will be.

5 Turn the outside of the vase to the desired shape and hollow out the inside.

6 With the half-finished vase still securely attached to the chuck, remove it completely from the lathe and put it carefully to one side (unless you have a second lathe available).

FIG 9.22
The padauk block and sycamore veneers, sandwiched, glued and clamped.

Attach a wooden faceplate to the lathe and glue the padauk composite block to its centre using superglue.

7 Rough down to a cylinder and *very roughly* shape the neck. At the end furthest from the headstock, cut a spigot with a diameter exactly the same as that of the vase opening where the neck is to be inserted.

8 Part off approximately 55mm ($2\frac{1}{8}$ in) back from the spigot. This will be the length of the neck.

9 Remount the half-finished vase on the lathe and glue the neck into the opening (see Fig 9.23).

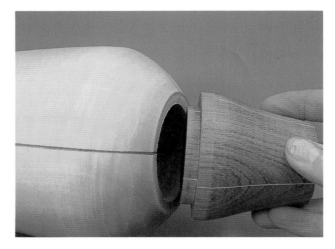

FIG 9.23
Insert the neck into the opening at the top of the vase and glue in position.

10 When the glue has dried, drill a hole through the neck and, using a hollowing tool, complete the shaping of the inside of the neck.

11 Shape the outside of the neck to blend in with the body.

12 Sand and finish, and part off. The total length of the vase including the neck should be 235mm ($9\frac{1}{4}$in).

13 Remount the wooden faceplate with the remainder of the padauk blank still glued to it. Turn a base with a recess of the appropriate size to take the bottom of the vase. Sand, finish and part off.

14 Glue the vase into the base.

Fig 9.24 shows the finished vase.

SMALL VENEERED BOX

The starting point for this project is the remaining pieces from the two blanks in the previous project. There should be enough wood left on each chuck to make the body and lid of a small box (see Fig 9.25).

METHOD

1 The remains of the padauk blank attached to the wooden faceplate on the lathe will become the box lid. Cut a spigot at one end 5mm ($\frac{3}{16}$in) deep and 61mm ($2\frac{3}{8}$in) in diameter. Cut away the inside of the spigot slightly, to produce a concave area. This will form the inside of the lid (see Fig 9.26). Sand and finish, and part off.

FIG 9.25
Starting point: the remaining pieces from the two composite blanks used in the previous project.

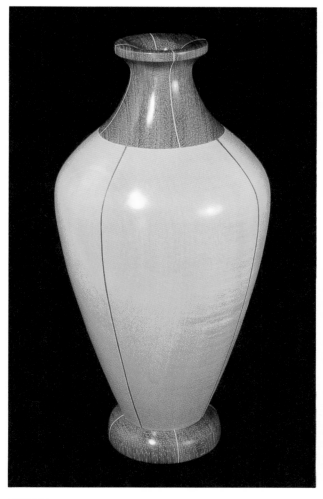

FIG 9.24
The finished vase, showing a strong colour contrast between the two timbers used.

FIG 9.26
Form a slightly concave spigot on the padauk blank, to make the inside of the lid.

FIG 9.27
Push the spigot firmly into the neck opening, which has been made to exactly the right size.

2   Remount the remains of the sycamore blank, still attached to its chuck, on to the lathe.

3   Shape the outside of the box, then hollow out the inside. Make sure that the neck opening is exactly the right size to take the spigot on the lid. A very tight fit is desirable at this stage (it will probably loosen later as the wood contracts slightly, but if not, gentle hand sanding will ease the fit). Sand and finish the inside.

4   Push the spigot of the lid firmly into the neck opening (see Fig 9.27).

5   Shape the outside of the lid, then sand and finish.

Fig 9.28 shows the finished box.

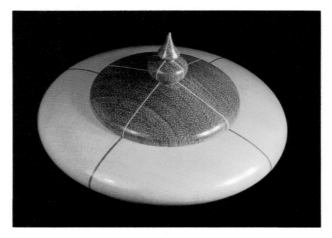

FIG 9.28
The finished box – a striking design.

FIG 9.29
Starting point: a padauk bowl-blank and sycamore veneers.

VENEERED PADAUK BOWL

The starting point for this project is a padauk bowl-blank 51mm (2in) deep and 255mm (10in) in diameter, plus three pieces of sycamore veneer 255mm (10in) long and 51mm (2in) wide (see Fig 9.29).

METHOD

1   Using a bandsaw, cut right through the padauk blank in three places. The precise position of the cuts is not crucial and is a matter of personal taste. This particular padauk bowl-blank had a small area of cream-coloured sap- wood at one edge. This was taken into account when the cuts were made, placing them opposite the sapwood in order to give the bowl 'balance'.

FIG 9.30
Reassemble the bowl-blank with the veneers sandwiched in place.

2   Glue the pieces back together, with the sycamore veneers sandwiched in between (see Fig 9.30).

3   When the glue has dried, mount the bowl-blank in the usual way and turn the underside. The bowl shown here was given a recessed foot and a rim of 33mm (1¼in). Sand and finish (see Fig 9.31).

4   Reverse-chuck the bowl and turn the inside, then sand and finish.

Fig 9.32 shows the finished bowl.

FIG 9.31
The underside of the bowl, turned and finished.

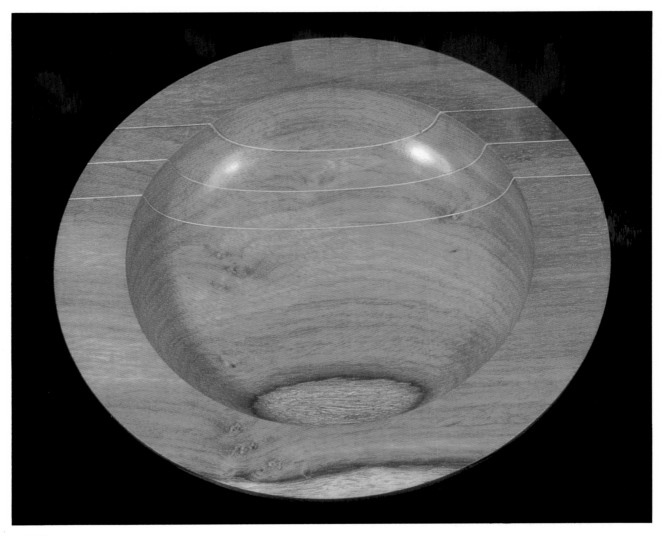

FIG 9.32
The finished bowl – note the area of sapwood, which 'balances' the three strips of veneer.

10

STICKWORK

◆ Safety ◆ Precision ◆ Adhesives ◆ Techniques ◆

PROJECTS

◆ Square-section stickwork ◆ Diamond stickwork ◆

ESSENTIAL EQUIPMENT

Basic turning tools and materials
Bandsaw
Strong wood adhesive
Assorted clamps

RECOMMENDED EQUIPMENT

Planer-thicknesser
(essential for diamond stickwork)
Table saw
Disc sander

Stickwork is not a new technique – indeed, examples can be found dating back to the nineteenth century. The technique is based on the principle of gluing together sticks, or rods, of different-coloured timbers into a composite block, and turning this block on the lathe. The patterns produced by the different colours can be very attractive and unusual. The number of different colours chosen is not critical – two would work quite well if the colours were strictly alternated, although it is more usual to see examples where three or more colours have been combined. It is an excellent way of using up small offcuts of timber which might otherwise be thrown away.

The process of constructing the composite block is rather labour intensive, so many people choose to rough down the finished block to a cylinder and then slice this into a number of discs for use in inlay work. In this way, the time and effort which has gone into making the block is put to good use over a period of time to decorate a large number of different items. However, you can also use the block to turn any three-dimensional item in the usual way, and some interesting colour patterns will emerge, as illustrated by the first project in this chapter.

SAFETY

The techniques described in this chapter involve the use of cutting machinery, such as bandsaws and table saws. Although these are not dangerous in themselves, it is nevertheless important to minimize potential hazards by taking all possible safety precautions.

All blades should be guarded and fingers kept well away from moving parts. Since very small pieces of wood are being cut, it is wise to construct some method of passing the wood through the blades while keeping your fingers well away. In order to achieve this, some form of jig should be constructed to enable the wood to be carried safely through the blades. One such jig, for use in conjunction with a table saw, is illustrated on page 103 (see Fig 10.18).

PRECISION

In order to achieve the best results, it is important to ensure that all the surfaces to be adhered are completely flat and free of any uneven patches. As already explained for laminates, failure to do so will result in gaps between adjacent surfaces, and these will show. Tiny gaps can be filled later with a suitable filler so that they are *barely* noticeable, but larger gaps will definitely show, even when filled. Consequently, all surfaces must be sanded or planed meticulously before assembly.

ADHESIVES

The same comments as for laminates apply to adhesives for stickwork, and I would recommend Cascamite to reduce the tendency for the layers to 'creep' during drying.

When gluing the rods together, do not try to glue too many together in one go. It is better to glue them in pairs, let the glue dry, then glue a few pairs together, let them dry, and so on. By building up successively in this way, you are more likely to achieve accurate assembly than if you try to glue all the rods at once.

TECHNIQUES

The projects in this chapter demonstrate two different stickwork techniques. The first method of assembly uses rods of square cross-section, resulting in chequerboard patterns on the end grain. This is the easiest of the two techniques in terms of both cutting and assembly. The second method is rather more complex, since it involves cutting thin rods at a precise angle along their length, and assembling them with considerable precision. The resulting geometric patterns are similar to those produced in patchwork.

SQUARE-SECTION STICKWORK

In this project, a composite block derived from square-section rods is used in two ways. Part of it is turned on the lathe into an apple, to illustrate the patterns produced in a three-dimensional object. The remainder is sawn into disc-shaped slices for use in inlay work.

EQUIPMENT

In addition to the essential equipment listed at the beginning of the chapter, a disc sander will be helpful for sanding the surfaces prior to gluing. This can be made simply by gluing a circular sheet of abrasive paper to a wooden disc screwed to a faceplate on the lathe. When the lathe is switched on, the disc rotates and the wood can be held against it (see Fig 10.1).

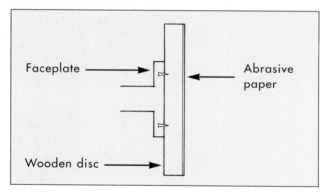

FIG 10.1
A home-made disc sander.

STARTING POINT

The starting point for this project is a number of square-section rods in different timbers, each approximately 10mm ($\frac{3}{8}$ in) square and 120mm ($4\frac{3}{4}$ in) long. The number you use (49 in this example) will determine the overall diameter of the composite cylinder. The range of colours is immaterial, and will be determined largely by availability. The rods are assembled more or less at random, so no precise geometric pattern is required.

In this example, lace-bobbin blanks were used simply because a large number were available in different timbers, and it seemed a good way of using them. They also formed a ready-made stock of sawn rods of approximately the right size. (It is worth remembering, however, that lace-bobbin blanks are not necessarily all exactly the same width, meaning that rather more sanding must be done prior to each stage of gluing.)

If lace-bobbin blanks are not available, the rods can be simply and quickly sawn to size on the bandsaw from any offcuts which you may have available. Fig 10.2 shows a few of the rods which were used in this project.

FIG 10.2
A selection of the lace-bobbin blanks used in this project.

METHOD

1   When you have collected together all the rods, the first stage is to glue them up. Place the rods together in pairs. Sand one surface of each rod, making sure that it is quite smooth, and then glue the sanded surfaces together. Clamp and leave to dry. (The number of pairs you will be able to glue at any one time will depend upon the number of clamps you have available.)

2   When the glue has dried, place the glued pairs side by side. Sand the appropriate surfaces, and then glue together (see Fig 10.3). Clamp and leave to dry. Repeat until you have several flat, rectangular composites.

3   Sand the surfaces of each rectangle on the disc sander, glue them together and clamp (see Fig 10.4). In this way, you will eventually achieve a solid block (see Fig 10.5).

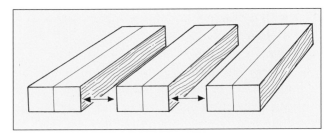

FIG 10.3
Glue pairs of rods together side by side.

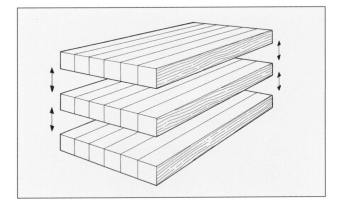

FIG 10.4
Glue the flat, rectangular composites together.

FIG 10.5
The finished composite blank.

TIP

The assembly does not necessarily have to be done in the way described, but the advantage is that it is easier and quicker to sand a large, flat surface than several narrow ones. When gluing up, try to ensure that the edges of the rods line up and that no rods of the same colour are placed next to each other. These are not vital considerations, but they do improve the overall effect.

4   Mount the block on the lathe and turn down to a cylinder (see Fig 10.6).

Fig 10.7 shows an apple turned from the block, while Fig 10.8 shows a slice taken from the remainder, ready for inlaying.

FIG 10.6
Turn down the composite block to a cylinder.

FIG 10.7
An apple turned from the composite block.

FIG 10.8
A slice cut from the remainder of the blank, ready to be used for inlaying.

DIAMOND STICKWORK

This project is similar in principle to the previous one, but rather more challenging. In this case, the sticks have a diamond-shaped cross-section instead of a square one, and when glued up the resulting cylinder will produce slices with a diamond 'patchwork' pattern rather than the chequerboard design in the previous project.

The process of producing the diamond-shaped rods is described in detail below, but be warned that it is not an easy one, and can take a long time. Because of this, the cylinder produced is perhaps best used to produce slices for inlaying. A three-dimensional object (such as the apple in the previous project) can, of course, be made, but this will use up a whole cylinder.

The results produced by this technique are really very attractive and unusual, and well worth the time and effort.

EQUIPMENT

For this project, access to a planer-thicknesser is strongly recommended. In addition, you will need a table saw with a blade-angling facility for cutting the diamond-shaped rods. If a table saw is not available, the cutting can be carried out on a bandsaw with a tilting table, although this is more difficult. Some experience in the use of this cutting machinery is advised before embarking on the cutting procedure.

THE CONSTRUCTION PRINCIPLE

The aim of the method described here is to produce a large number of diamond-shaped rods of equal dimensions, which can be assembled lengthways into a roughly cylindrical shape ready for turning on the lathe. The type of pattern produced will depend on two factors:

1   The juxtaposition of different colours. In the previous project, where lace-bobbin blanks were used, this was not critical, but with diamond stickwork the visual impact is enhanced if the colours are arranged in some kind of regular pattern, so give this a little thought beforehand. One possibility is to arrange the rods so that no two of the same colour are touching, thereby maximizing the effect of the colour contrasts (see Fig 10.9). An alternative is to arrange the colours in bands radiating out from the centre (see Fig 10.10). It is worthwhile experimenting with different patterns before gluing up.

FIG 10.9
Colours arranged in an alternating pattern.

FIG 10.10
Colours arranged in radiating bands.

2 The shape of the diamonds. The diamonds can be cut into either 45°/135° shapes (see Fig 10.11) or 60°/120° shapes (see Fig 10.12). In Figs 10.9 and 10.10 the diamonds are 45°/135°.

If 60°/120° shapes are cut, a slightly different pattern will be created (see Fig 10.13).

In this project, 45°/135° diamonds are used.

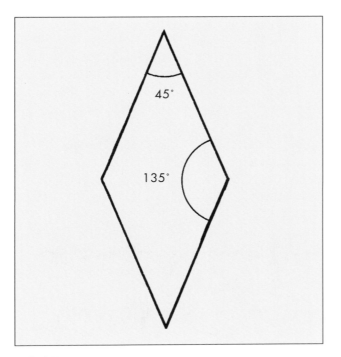

FIG 10.11
Diamond cross-section using angles of 45° and 135°.

FIG 10.13
The pattern created using 60°/120° diamonds.

IMPORTANT CONSIDERATIONS

It is absolutely essential that all the diamond rods are of *exactly* the right dimensions. If they are not, they will not fit together. You will, therefore, need to take time to ensure that:

- For each diamond rod cut, the opposite angles are precisely 45° and 135° (see Fig 10.14).

- All four sides of the diamond are equal in length (Fig 10.15).

- All the rods are exactly the same in all dimensions.

- All the surfaces are planed smooth, with no uneven patches.

To achieve the level of accuracy required, it is advisable to carry out all the cutting procedures in one go. In other words, make all the initial cuts on the bandsaw and do all the planer-thicknessing during the same work session. Likewise, do all the

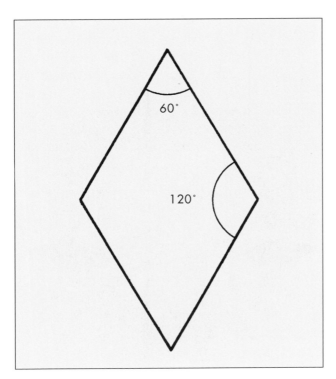

FIG 10.12
Diamond cross-section using angles of 60° and 120°.

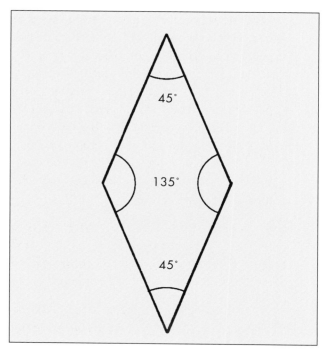

FIG 10.14
The opposite angles of the diamond must be exactly 45° and 135° respectively.

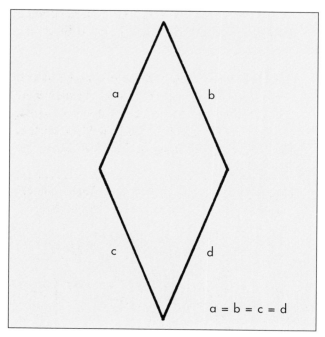

FIG 10.15
All four sides of the diamond must be equal in length.

cutting on the table saw in one go. In this way, you will ensure that the equipment is adjusted to make consistent cuts.

STARTING POINT

The starting point for this project is several small planks of different-coloured timbers. In this example, five different timbers were used, but this number is not critical – three, four or six would work equally well. The number of different timbers used will depend on the overall effect desired, and the availability of timbers of contrasting colours.

The length of the planks does not matter, but they should be long enough to pass through the planer-thicknesser. The width should be approximately 100mm (4in), and the depth approximately 30mm ($1\frac{1}{4}$in). These dimensions are not critical at this stage, as all the planks will be sawn and planed to *exactly* the same width and thickness.

Make sure that you have more than enough wood for the project, since extra pieces of the same dimensions will be needed for setting up the table saw. These will be wasted.

MATERIALS AND METHOD

Sticky tape

1   Using the bandsaw, cut each plank of wood to exactly the width of the narrowest plank. In this example, it is 100mm (4in).

The width of the planks becomes the length of the rods, and therefore the length of the finished cylinder. Obviously, the longer the cylinder, the more you will be able to make out of it. However, if you make it too long, it can be difficult to glue the rods together, so you need to aim for an optimum length: 100mm (4in) is a good compromise (see Fig 10.16).

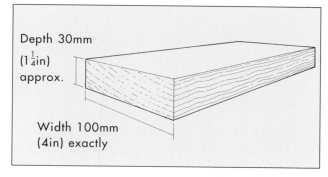

FIG 10.16
The width of the plank becomes the length of each rod, and hence the length of the composite cylinder.

The planks do not need to be all the same length. The longer the plank, the more rods can be cut from it. Since an equal number of different colours is not necessary, the longer the planks the better.

2   Plane one side of each plank. In this example, you now have five planks of equal width, all planed on one side.

3   Adjust the bandsaw blade to give a cut of the appropriate width. This width will determine the overall cross-section size of the diamond rods. In this example, the width was 6mm ($\frac{1}{4}$in). Cut the plank *slightly* oversize to allow for thicknessing.

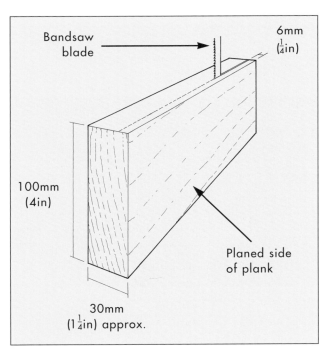

FIG 10.17
Pass the blank through the bandsaw sideways, ensuring that the planed side is cut off.

4   Pass each plank through the bandsaw blade once, ensuring that the *planed* side is cut off (see Fig 10.17). This will produce five thin rectangles, each in a different colour. Each rectangle will have one planed side and one unplaned side.

5   Plane one side of the remainder of each plank, and repeat step 4.

6   Repeat steps 2 and 4 until no more thin rectangles can be produced. The number will depend on the depth of the original planks and the depth of the rectangles you have cut. In this example, the original planks were approximately 30mm ($1\frac{1}{4}$in) deep, so each one produced three thin rectangles. If your original planks were very thin (e.g. approximately 8mm/$\frac{5}{16}$in) you will not need to pass them the bandsaw: just pass each one through the planer-thicknesser.

7   You should now have a collection of thin rectangles 100mm (4in) wide, and 6mm ($\frac{1}{4}$in) deep, possibly of varying lengths. Each rectangle will be planed on one side only.

8   Pass each rectangle through the thicknesser, so that each unplaned side now becomes planed and all the rectangles are exactly the same thickness. Place the rectangles on one side while you set up the table saw.

9   The table saw blade should be angled to make a cut of 45°. At this stage, get it as accurate as you can – fine tuning will have to be done a little later.

10   Because you will be cutting very small pieces of wood, it is important to construct a carrier jig, which slides on the surface of the table saw to pass the wood safely through the blade without endangering your fingers. Fig 10.18 shows one

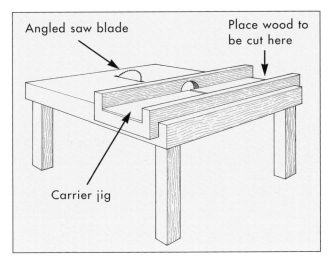

FIG 10.18
One possible arrangement for a table saw with carrier jig.

possible arrangement, but feel free to adapt this to suit your own purposes. Ideally, the blade should be guarded. In order to reveal the construction details, there is no blade guard in place in the diagram.

11 Test the saw blade angle in order to adjust it to precisely the correct position. It is possible, but unlikely, that you will have adjusted it to the correct angle first time round, and unfortunately the only way to find out is by trial and error. You will need to cut and assemble some sample diamond rods in order to discover the accuracy of fit. Do not use the rectangles which you have already carefully prepared. Instead, use a length of scrap wood cut to the same dimensions.

12 Clamp the scrap wood on to the carrier jig on the table saw, and pass it through the blade so that the end is sawn off at an angle of approximately 45° (see Fig 10.19).

13 It was stressed earlier that each diamond rod must have all four sides the same length, and this too is achieved through trial and error. Bolt a small piece of scrap wood on to the front end of the carrier jig to act as a 'width-stop'. Place it so as to produce a diamond rod with equal sides (see Fig 10.20). Push the sawn end of the scrap wood against it.

14 Pass the wood through the blade to cut off the first rod (see Figs 10.21 and 10.22). Repeat, to produce two rods with diamond-shaped cross-sections.

15 Place the two rods together side by side and check that the adjacent sides are of equal length (see Fig 10.23). (It is a good idea to swap the ends round to check the fit in the other direction as well.) If you are very lucky, the sides will fit exactly, which will tell you that all the sides are the same length. However, it is more likely that they will not be. Adjust the position of the width-stop accordingly. Repeat this procedure until you are satisfied that the width-stop is correctly positioned to produce rods with sides of exactly equal length. This may take several

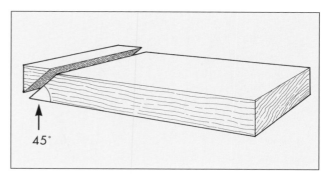

FIG 10.19
Saw off the end of the scrap wood at an angle of 45°.

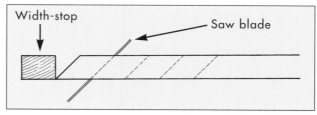

FIG 10.20
A piece of scrap wood bolted to the carrier jig acts as a width-stop.

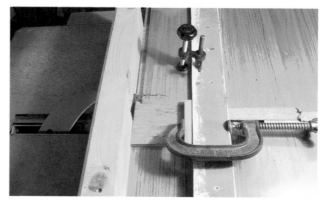

FIG 10.21
The table saw and makeshift carrier jig.

FIG 10.22
Use the saw to cut off the first diamond rod.

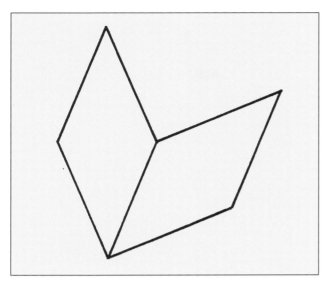

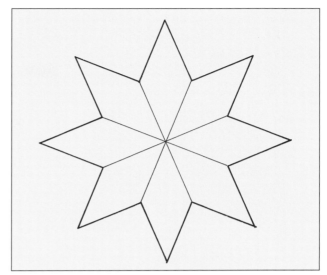

FIG 10.23
Place two diamond rods side by side lengthways: the sides should match exactly.

goes, but it is a crucial procedure, since if the sides are not equal the rods will not fit together. Even a very small discrepancy will produce quite a large gap eventually, because any inaccuracy will be multiplied by eight when gluing up eight rods to form a circle.

16 Now pass the scrap wood through the blade eight times, to produce eight diamond rods.

17 Glue these together lengthways into a circle (see Figs 10.24 and 10.25). (In Fig 10.25, woods of two different colours have been assembled in alternating positions, for added clarity.) Hold the segments in place with sticky tape until the glue has dried.

18 It should now be possible to determine the accuracy of your angle of cut. If you are very lucky, and have set the saw blade to exactly 45°, your segments will fit perfectly. It is more likely, though, that you will have a less than perfect fit – you should be able to see whether the blade angle is slightly too big or slightly too small. Adjust it accordingly and cut eight more pieces. Assemble them as before and see if the fit is any better. Repeat this procedure until the segments fit together perfectly. There should be no gaps, and all the points should meet in the middle. When this

FIGS 10.24 AND 10.25
Glue the diamond rods into a circle as shown, using sticky tape to hold them in place.

has been achieved, your table saw is at precisely the right angle, and your width-stop is in exactly the right place, so you are ready to cut the pieces which you prepared earlier!

19 Collect together all the prepared thin rectangles and pass them one by one through the table saw, as described above. This will give you a number of diamond rods in different colours, ready for assembly (see Fig 10.26).

20 Having decided how the colours are to be arranged, begin gluing pairs together. When dry, assemble four pairs into a circle, as described in step 17.

FIG 10.26
Sort the rods into piles of different colours, ready for assembly.

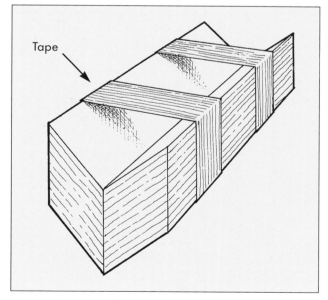

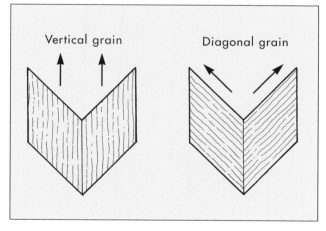

FIG 10.28
The grain of a pair of rods may run vertically or diagonally.

FIG 10.27
Glue up a pair of rods and hold them in place with sticky tape until the glue has dried.

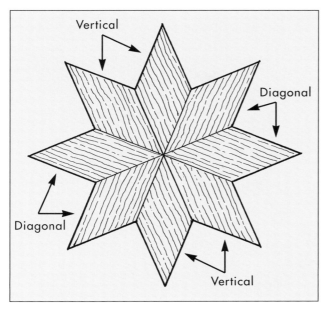

FIG 10.29
Assemble the pairs of rods so that the grain direction alternates between vertical and diagonal.

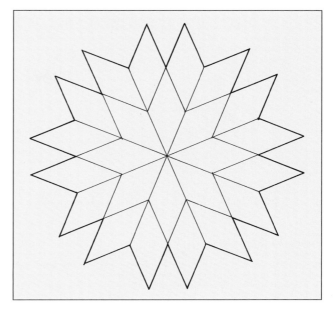

FIG 10.30
Glue the second layer of rods in position.

TIP

When gluing up the pairs of rods, secure them with sticky tape until the glue has dried, as shown in Fig 10.27.

Before gluing up, try to match the direction of the grain in each segment. Look at the end face of each segment: the grain runs in one of two directions – either straight up and down, or diagonally (see Fig 10.28). To get the best results from your assembly, match each pair so that the end grain runs in the same direction. When you join up your four pairs to form a circle, the grain direction should alternate with each pair (see Fig 10.29), and this will enhance the general appearance. However, this only matters if there is a strongly visible grain. If the grain is barely visible, matching the grain direction is not really necessary.

21 When the glue is dry, carefully remove all the surplus glue from the sides of the segments, so that all the surfaces are clean. Failure to do so will result in misalignment.

22 Glue the second layer of segments in place (see Fig 10.30).

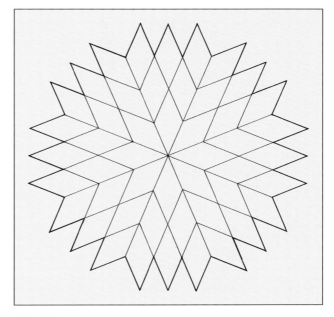

FIG 10.31
Glue the third layer of rods in position.

23 Continue in this way until you have a roughly cylindrical shape with a star-shaped edge (see Fig 10.31). The thickness of this cylinder will depend on the desired diameter of the slices you ultimately wish to use, and the number of rods you have available.

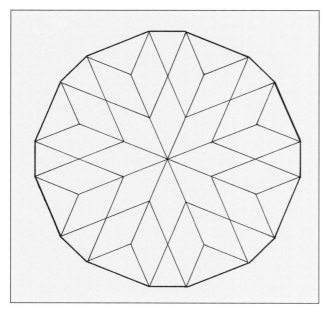

FIG 10.32
The gaps around the edge can be filled with rods of small triangular cross-section.

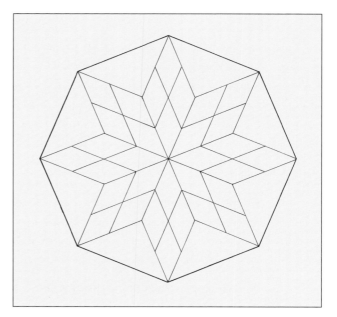

FIG 10.33
By altering the pattern of the diamond rods, larger triangles can be incorporated into the gaps around the edge.

24   Fill in the gaps between the points around the edge with small triangular pieces of wood cut to the right size and shape (see Fig 10.32). By altering the assembled pattern of segments, larger triangles can be incorporated into the gaps, creating a larger cylinder (see Fig 10.33). Alternatively, the points can be left on and simply turned off on the lathe, although this is somewhat wasteful.

25   When the glue has dried, mount the cylinder on the lathe, and rough down to a true cylinder. Slices can now be taken from this as required.

TIP

It is best to cut your slices from the cylinder as and when you need them. The thickness required will depend on the use to which they are to be put.

Fig 10.34 shows an example of a disc-shaped slice ready for inlaying. Fig 10.35 shows an example of a box with a diamond stickwork slice inlaid into the lid.

FIG 10.34
A slice cut from the composite cylinder, ready to be used for inlaying.

FIG 10.35
A circular box, with the lid inlaid with a diamond stickwork slice.

CUTTING DISCS FOR INLAYING

Discs can be cut from the cylindrical block with the lathe running, using a narrow parting tool. An alternative method, which is less wasteful, is to cut the slices on the bandsaw, but in order to do this accurately and safely you will need to construct a simple carrier.

METHOD

1   Take a short piece of square-section plastic drainpipe, approximately 50mm (2in) longer than your cylindrical block. Cut this in half lengthways on the diagonal (see Fig 10.36).

2   Reassemble the drainpipe as shown in Fig 10.37. Place the cylindrical block inside the makeshift carrier so that it fits snugly (see Fig 10.38) – it may be necessary to cut down the drainpipe still further, depending on the dimensions of your cylinder.

3   When the cylinder is safely secured inside the carrier, pass the whole construction through the bandsaw, cutting off a slice to the desired thickness. Since the drainpipe is plastic, it will not damage the bandsaw blade. The excess length of pipe can be used as a 'handle', to enable you to slice right down to the very end of the block with no wastage at all.

ALTERNATIVE PATTERNS

It is possible to incorporate squares into the diamond pattern. This will give a slightly different geometric design and, if you find it difficult to cut the diamonds, it means that you can make them go a little further by interspersing them with square sections, which are easier to cut. Fig 10.39 shows one possible arrangement. It is worth spending a little time sketching out a series of possible patterns before you begin.

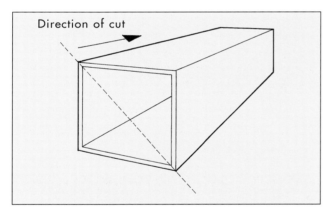

FIG 10.36
Cut corner to corner from one end to the other.

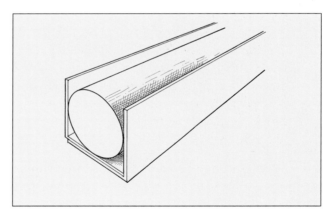

FIG 10.38
The cylindrical block should fit snugly in the carrier.

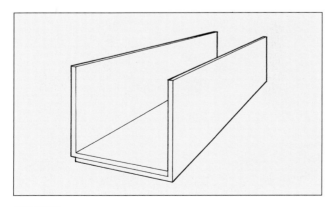

FIG 10.37
Assemble the two L-shapes to form a carrier.

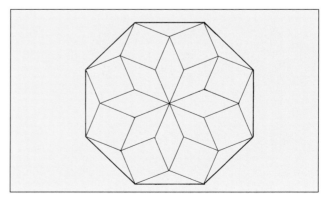

FIG 10.39
Diamonds and squares used in combination.

11

INLAYING WOOD BANDINGS AND PLUGS

◆ Wood bandings ◆ Wooden plugs ◆ Selection of timber ◆

PROJECTS

◆ Mirror-surround inlaid with wood banding ◆ Cylindrical box inlaid with black banding ◆
◆ Mirror-surround inlaid with wooden plugs ◆

ESSENTIAL EQUIPMENT

Sharp knife
Plug cutter
Mini-hacksaw
Drill
Superglue
Basic turning tools and materials

Wood bandings are readily available from various suppliers, and wooden plugs are very easy to cut from odd scraps of wood. Consequently, both are extremely easy methods of inlaying and can look very attractive. Special equipment is not required, nor is a high level of skill.

WOOD BANDINGS

These thin composite strips are available in an excellent range of patterns and colours (see Fig 11.1). They are approximately 0.7mm (0.0315in) thick, and range in width from 1mm ($\frac{1}{32}$in) up to approximately 6mm ($\frac{1}{4}$in). Suppliers of woodturning accessories usually sell them in metre lengths, the price varying according to width and the timbers used within the banding.

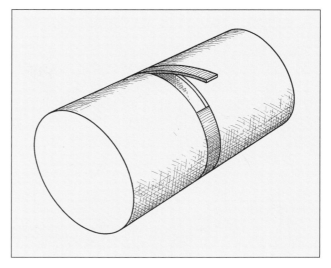

FIG 11.2
Glue the banding into the groove, cut to the correct width and depth using a parting tool or similar.

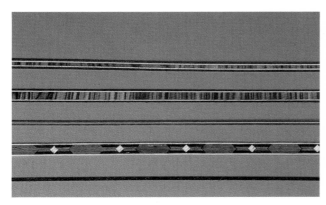

FIG 11.1
Wood bandings are available in a range of colours, patterns and sizes.

The most common method of inlay is simply to cut a groove with a suitable-sized tool (a parting tool or similar), making sure that it is exactly the right width and depth for the chosen banding, and then glue the banding in place around the groove (see Fig 11.2) – superglue is recommended, because of the fast setting time. Fig 11.3 shows a sycamore box, with wood banding inlaid around the side of the lid using this method.

This technique is extremely quick and simple, because the banding is inlaid in the same plane as the rotation and the groove can therefore be cut with the lathe running. In addition, the banding can be inlaid all in one strip. Because this is such a straightforward method, and one with which most woodturners are familiar, the projects in this

FIG 11.3
A cylindrical box inlaid with wood banding.

chapter illustrate two alternative inlay techniques, both of which are less common. They take rather longer, but create quite different effects.

WOODEN PLUGS

These small cylinders of wood can be cut quickly and easily from any piece of scrap wood, using a plug cutter (see Fig 11.4). This device fits into a normal drill chuck and can be used with an ordinary hand-held drill or a pillar drill. When the drill is switched on and the plug cutter inserted into the surface of the wood, a small cylinder is cut neatly into the surface. This process is repeated as often as necessary to produce the required number of plugs. The size of the plugs can be varied according to the size of the plug cutter. The plugs are then removed by lifting them out from their base using a screwdriver or similar tool (they break away easily from the surface). In this way, a large number of plugs can be cut in a matter of minutes – a useful way of using up odd scraps of wood, which are perhaps too small to be used for anything else. The plugs can be stored for later use.

Wooden plugs are inlaid by first drilling holes with the same diameter as that of the plugs, then gluing the plugs into the holes so that the tops are just proud of the surface (see Fig 11.5). The plugs are then cut flush with the surface using the appropriate turning tool.

FIG 11.4
A plug cutter.

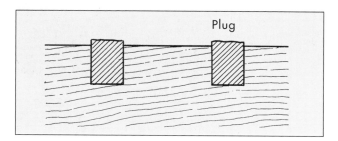

FIG 11.5
Glue the plugs into the holes so that their tops are just proud of the surface of the wood.

SELECTION OF TIMBER

As with any composite or inlay technique, it is advisable to select timbers which contrast strongly with the colour of the main piece. The 'exotic' timbers, such as purpleheart, padauk, kingwood and rosewood are all highly suitable, and contrast well with paler timbers. Where a dark wood forms the main item, paler inlays such as sycamore, holly and amarello would provide a good contrast.

MIRROR-SURROUND INLAID WITH WOOD BANDING

The starting point for this project is a partially finished mirror-surround in mahogany. (This particular piece of wood was salvaged from a rubbish tip and had originally formed the lid of a lavatory seat!) It is 324mm ($12\frac{3}{4}$in) in diameter, with a depth of 16mm ($\frac{5}{8}$in). The rim is 47mm ($1\frac{7}{8}$in) wide, and the recess in the centre (which will receive the mirror glass) is 230mm (9in) in diameter. The recess is approximately 2.5mm ($\frac{1}{8}$in) deep (see Fig 11.6).

FIG 11.6
Starting point: a mahogany mirror-surround, with a recess ready to take the mirror glass.

A groove 5.5mm ($\frac{1}{4}$in) wide and 1mm ($\frac{1}{32}$in) deep has been cut in the surface of the rim to receive the banding, which has the same dimensions. Fig 11.7 shows how the groove is cut using a small parting tool: it is important to ensure that the width and depth of the groove exactly matches the banding.

A decorative dovetail recess has been cut on the back of the surround, so that it can be remounted easily on to an expanding dovetail collet.

MATERIALS AND METHOD

Wood banding

Flexible adhesive (e.g. silicone sealant)

Mirror

1   As the banding is to be inlaid in a flat plane, it cannot be inserted all in one piece because it will not bend sideways. Consequently, it must be cut into short lengths and each piece inserted individually. Cut the banding into 26mm (1in) lengths, using a sharp blade and cutting at regular intervals along the pattern of the banding (see Fig 11.8).

The length of these pieces is critical. They need to be as long as possible so that you do not have to fiddle around with more of them than necessary. At the same time, if they are too long they will not fit neatly into the groove. Try to angle the edges slightly, so that they fit flush together (see Fig 11.9).

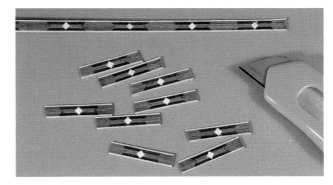

FIG 11.8
Cut the banding into small pieces, cutting at regular intervals along the pattern.

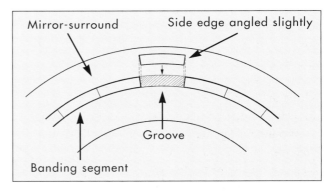

FIG 11.9
Angle the edges of the banding segments very slightly so that they will fit flush together in the groove.

2   Insert the pieces into the groove one at a time. They should fit tightly in place. When you get to the last two or three pieces of banding, it may be necessary to cut them down in size slightly so that they fit exactly. It is therefore important not to glue all the pieces in place before you have finished (see Fig 11.10).

FIG 11.7
Cut the groove for the banding, using a small parting tool.

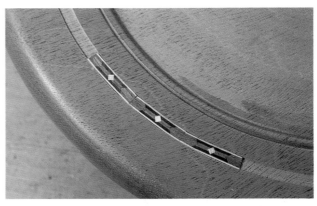

FIG 11.10
Insert pieces of banding into the groove.

3   When all the pieces have been placed in position, apply some of the intended finish (e.g. sanding sealer) to the area. When this has dried, trickle a small amount of thin superglue over the banding to bond it securely in place – the sealer will prevent the glue staining and discolouring the wood.

4   Remount the surround on to the lathe and, with the lathe running, sand the entire surface. The banding will then be completely flush with the surface of the surround. Apply the desired finish in the usual way; in this example, sanding sealer and carnauba wax were used.

5   Finally, glue the mirror glass into the recess. A flexible adhesive, such as a silicone sealant, should be used for this. The wood may shrink over time, and a flexible adhesive will move with it. If a brittle drying adhesive is used, there is a danger that the glass may crack.

Fig 11.11 shows the finished mirror. Fig 11.12 shows another one in lime, with two rings of banding.

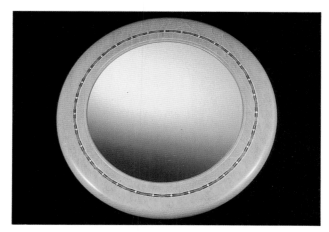

FIG 11.11
The finished mirror, complete with decorative banding.

FIG 11.12
A similar mirror but this time with two rings of banding.

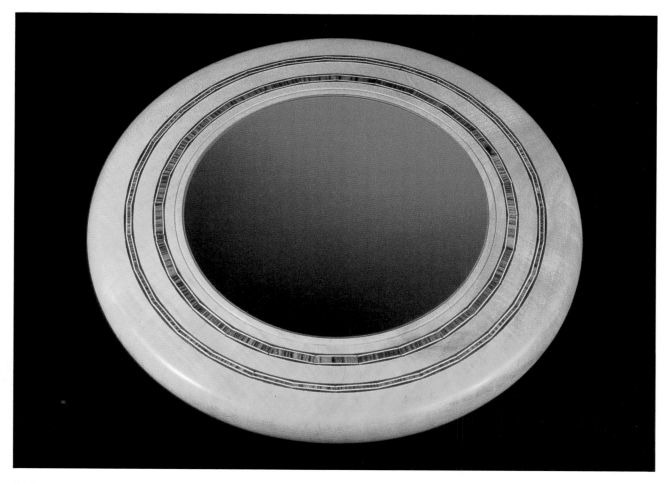

CYLINDRICAL BOX INLAID WITH BLACK BANDING

The starting point for this project is a cylindrical amarello box, which has been turned and sanded but has not had any finish applied. It has not yet been parted off, and is still attached to the remainder of the blank. The box is 87mm ($3\frac{7}{8}$in) long, with a diameter of 65mm ($2\frac{1}{2}$in) and lid length of 31mm ($1\frac{1}{4}$in). The top of the lid is slightly convex, and at this stage is fitted tightly to the body (see Fig 11.13). The box is to be inlaid with very thin black banding, 1mm ($\frac{1}{32}$in) wide and 1mm ($\frac{1}{32}$in) deep.

FIG 11.13
Starting point: a cylindrical amarello box with a slightly convex lid.

MATERIALS AND METHOD

Sticky tape

Thin black banding

1   Divide the surface of the lid into six equal segments. This number was chosen because it is easy to divide a circle into six. Measure the radius with a pair of compasses or dividers and then, using this distance, mark off a series of arcs around the circumference to divide it exactly into six (see Fig 11.14).

2   Mark in the lines with a pencil (see Fig 11.15).

3   Starting at the point at which one of the pencil lines meets the edge of the lid, take a piece of sticky tape and place it diagonally along the side of box (see Fig 11.16). Draw a

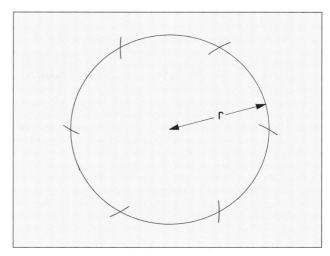

FIG 11.14
Divide the circumference of the circle by the radius to create six equidistant points.

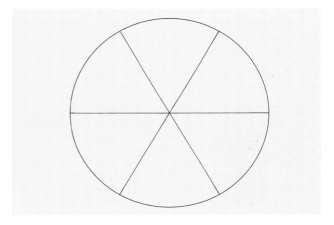

FIG 11.15
Draw in the intersecting lines to create six segments.

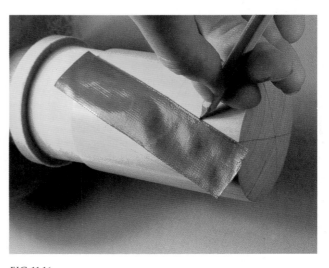

FIG 11.16
Draw in a pencil line along the edge of the sticky tape to mark the position of the first inlay.

pencil line along the edge of the tape to mark the position of the first inlay.

The precise angle of the first diagonal is not critical and is a matter of personal preference. Indeed, the line does not have to be diagonal at all. It could be absolutely vertical (perpendicular to the base of the box), in which case a rather different visual effect would be created.

4   Now move to the point at which the second pencil line meets the edge of the lid and repeat the process, making sure that the second diagonal line is *exactly parallel* to the first.

5   Repeat this all the way round, until all six diagonal lines have been drawn around the side of the box. The lines should meet exactly with the corresponding pencil lines on the top of the lid.

6   Using a mini-hacksaw with a blade width of 1mm ($\frac{1}{32}$ in), saw carefully along the pencil lines to a depth of exactly 1mm ($\frac{1}{32}$ in) (see Fig 11.17). Repeat with the pencil lines on the top of the lid. The grooves are now ready to receive the banding.

7   Apply the desired finish to the entire surface of the box – in this example, sanding sealer was used. This will prevent the glue discolouring the wood.

8   Remove the lid and push lengths of banding into the cut grooves in the body of the box. They should fit exactly. Trickle superglue carefully along the lengths of the inlays to secure them in place. Repeat this process with the grooves on the sides and top of the lid (see Fig 11.18).

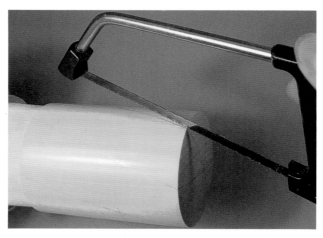

FIG 11.17
Saw carefully along the pencil lines to cut grooves to a depth of 1mm ($\frac{1}{32}$ in).

FIG 11.18
Inlay the banding into the grooves.

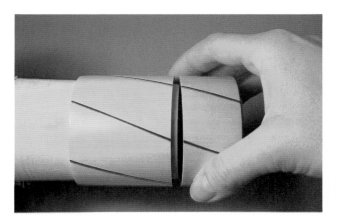

FIG 11.19
Replace the lid – the lines of banding should meet exactly.

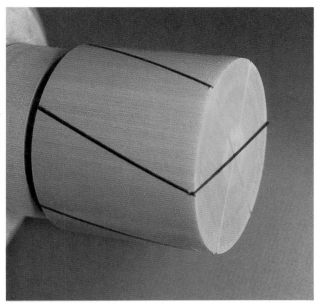

FIG 11.20
Inlay banding in the grooves in the base of the box.

9 When the glue has dried, sand the bottom half of the box, paying particular attention to the edge which will meet the lid. Replace the lid (see Fig 11.19) and sand.

10 Apply sanding sealer and carnauba wax, or any other preferred finish. Part off.

11 The final stage is not absolutely necessary, but it does add a nice finishing touch. Turn a spigot on the remainder of the blank, which is still attached to the chuck after the box has been parted off. The spigot should be the same diameter as the inside of the box. This will form a tight jam-chuck for reverse-chucking the body of the box.

12 Push the body of the box on to the spigot and check to see that it runs true. True-up the base of the box using a skew chisel.

13 With the lathe stationary, join up the ends of the banding lines (which meet the base) with a pencil and ruler. If the lines have been inlaid accurately, they should form a perfect star – to match the one on the top of the lid – and will meet exactly in the centre of the base. If your workmanship has been less than accurate, they won't!

14 Using the mini-hacksaw, cut along the lines as before, to create grooves of the correct width and depth. Glue the banding lines in place (see Fig 11.20).

15 Sand and polish the base.

Fig 11.21 shows the finished box.

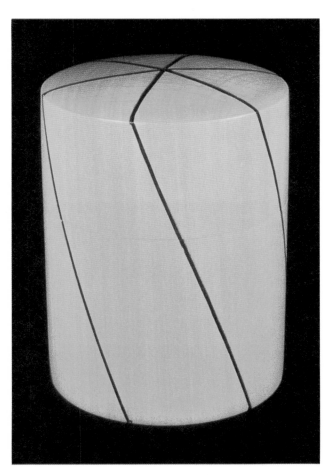

FIG 11.21
The finished box, demonstrating the importance of precise workmanship in achieving the desired effect.

117

MIRROR-SURROUND INLAID WITH WOODEN PLUGS

The starting point for this project is a lime mirror-surround 249mm ($9\frac{3}{4}$ in) in diameter, with a depth of 6mm ($\frac{1}{4}$ in) and a rim width of 48mm ($1\frac{7}{8}$ in). The recess for the glass is 153mm (6in) in diameter and 2mm ($\frac{1}{16}$ in) deep (see Fig 11.22). A dovetail recess has been cut into the back of the surround so that it can be remounted easily on to an expanding dovetail collet chuck.

Purpleheart and padauk were chosen for the plugs, as their attractive colours contrast well with the lime of the surround.

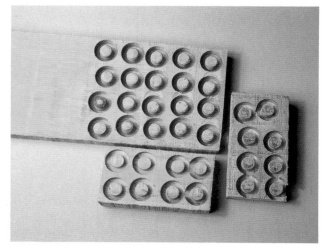

FIG 11.23
Cut plugs in scrap pieces of purpleheart and padauk, using a plug cutter.

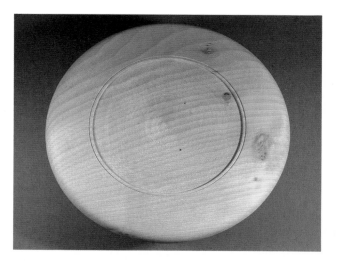

FIG 11.22
Starting point: a lime mirror-surround.

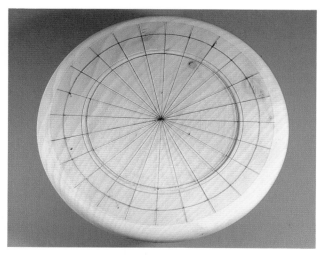

FIG 11.24
Mark out the mirror-surround into 24 equal segments, using a plastic template.

MATERIALS AND METHOD

Purpleheart and padauk for plugs

Flexible adhesive (e.g. silicone sealant)

Mirror

1   Using a 7mm ($\frac{1}{4}$ in) plug-cutter, cut a number of plugs in some scrap pieces of purpleheart and padauk (see Fig 11.23). Using the end of a screwdriver, gently ease the plugs from the surrounding wood.

2   Mark out the mirror-surround into 24 equal segments. In this example, a plastic template was used (see Fig 11.24). For details of how to make this template, see Chapter 2. Alternatively, an indexing ring (see Chapter 1) could have been used for marking out.

3   Using a 7mm ($\frac{1}{4}$ in) drill bit, drill holes at each of the 24 points to a depth slightly less than the length of the plugs.

4   Gently tap the plugs into the holes, alternating the purpleheart and padauk. The ends of the plugs will be slightly proud of the surface (see Fig 11.25). They should also be a good, tight fit.

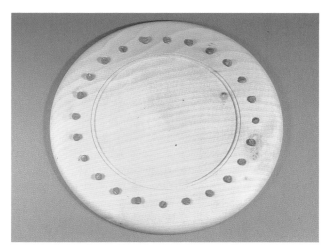

FIG 11.25
Insert the plugs into the holes – the ends will be slightly proud of the surface.

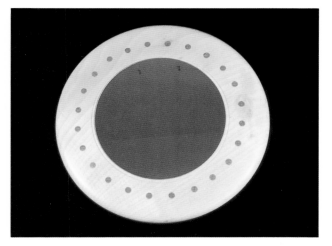

FIG 11.26
The finished mirror, complete with glass.

5   When all the plugs have been inserted, coat the surrounding area with sanding sealer, to prevent the glue discolouring the wood.

6   Trickle a small quantity of thin superglue around the edges of each plug to secure.

7   Remount the mirror-surround on the lathe and true-up the surface, so that any excess wood is removed. The plugs should now be completely flush with the surface.

8   Sand, then apply sanding sealer and carnauba wax, or any preferred finish.

9   Glue the glass into the recess using a flexible adhesive, such as silicone sealant.

Fig 11.26 shows the finished mirror, and Fig 11.27 the inlaid plugs in detail.

FIG 11.27
Detail of the inlaid plugs.

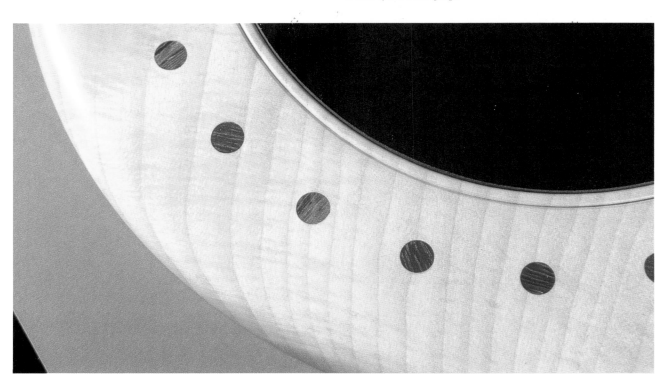

PART FOUR
MISCELLANEOUS TECHNIQUES

Resins

Scorching Techniques

Altering Surface Texture

Carving

INTRODUCTION

Far from being a discarded ragbag of unrelated ideas consigned to the end of the book, this last section does in fact include some of the most visually stunning and exciting techniques of all. The fact that they do not fit into any of the preceding sections, nor hang together as an alternative section with a distinct theme, certainly does not detract from their individual value.

Chapter 12 examines the use of polyester casting resins, which, when combined with pigments, can be poured into the holes, cracks, fissures and grooves of various turned items. Metallic powders can be added to the resins to create an attractive and unusual effect.

Chapter 13 explores different methods of scorching wood to alter the colour and texture of the surface. The use of pyrography tools and small gas torches is described, plus methods of cutting or drilling through scorched sections to create further patterns.

Chapter 14 looks at two of the many ways in which the surface texture of wood can be altered dramatically. The use of an automatic centre punch is described, and a little-known use of steaming is then combined with this technique to create a very unusual texture effect.

The last chapter illustrates three different carving methods. The first is chip carving, a simple technique which can be achieved using a sharp craft knife or Stanley knife. The simple patterns created by this method can be used to decorate a bowl rim or box lid very effectively. In the first project, a piercing saw is used to begin the process of carving a fret-work type edge around the rim of a sycamore platter. Then, carving 'in the round' along a system of geometric spiral lines is used to transform a simple oval box into a pineapple.

12
RESINS

◆ Safety ◆ Pigments ◆ Equipment ◆ Finishing ◆

PROJECTS

◆ Banksia nut embedded with gold-effect resin ◆ Yew bowl embedded with black resin ◆
◆ Yew bowl embedded with silver- and gold-effect resins ◆
◆ Padauk box decorated with ivory-coloured resin ◆

ESSENTIAL EQUIPMENT

Small plastic mixing pots and stirrers
Plenty of old rags and newspapers
Basic turning tools and materials

RECOMMENDED EQUIPMENT

Minicraft drill with glass-engraving cutter
attachment

Various types of polyester casting resins are available, and most come in the form of a clear, syrupy liquid. When a hardener is added, the liquid begins to turn solid, and will be completely hard in a matter of hours. As the name suggests, they are usually used for casting, and many people will have seen paperweights embedded with flowers and other similar ornaments at craft fairs. The versatility of casting resin, however, makes it ideal for decorative embedding in wood. This chapter explores some of the possibilities, including filling holes in banksia nuts, natural fissures in the surface of burr woods and pre-cut grooves.

Polyester resins are available from some craft shops, suppliers of sculptors' equipment and through mail order. Since there are many different types, all manufactured for different purposes, it is a good idea to discuss with the supplier which is the best for your particular use.

SAFETY

Polyester resins are not dangerous, but some simple, common-sense health and safety precautions should be observed when using them.

The resins, hardeners and pigments are highly flammable and should not be used close to a heat source, including cigarettes. There should be good ventilation in the workshop, since the fumes can cause dizziness and irritation if breathed in over a long period. When sanding hardened resin, use full respiratory protection. Contact with the skin should be avoided, as this can cause irritation in some people.

Metal fillers – especially aluminium powder, which can be highly combustible under certain conditions – should be stored safely away from heat and damp, and the lids should be kept tightly on the containers when not in use.

PIGMENTS

Various different pigments are available for mixing with the resin. These are mixed in thoroughly *before* the addition of the hardener.

Coloured pigments These are thick liquids or pastes which can be mixed directly with the resin by stirring, and only a small amount is needed. There are two types – opaque, and translucent. For the projects in this chapter I have used the opaque variety, because only small quantities of resin have been used, in specific areas. However, you might also like to consider the use of translucent pigments, which would allow the grain to remain visible beneath – when you have a larger area to fill, perhaps.

It is worth giving some careful thought to the colours to be used. In my opinion, it is usually a good idea to avoid unnatural, garish shades. I tend to use just black, ivory and metallic. However, this is, as always, a matter of personal taste.

Metal fillers These are finely powdered pure metals (not pigments) which, when mixed with resin, give a metallic appearance. They are available in aluminium (which gives a silver effect), brass (which gives a gold effect), copper, bronze and nickel-brass.

Each powder has a 'mesh' number, which refers to the fineness of the powder. The higher the mesh number, the finer the powder. Generally, you should buy the finest powder possible, because this will give the best effect. Most of the metal fillers supplied with the resins have a mesh number of 200–300, but art shops sometimes sell a good range of finer-mesh powders – around 800–900 – which can be mixed safely with resins, so it is worth shopping around.

Unlike coloured pigments, which only need a small quantity added to the resin, metal fillers need to be added in relatively large amounts. The proportions are roughly one part filler to one part resin by volume, but with slightly more filler: the result will be thick paste. If it is too thick to pour (this depends on the ambient temperature), it must be pushed into position. Gentle tapping will cause it to settle in, and any air bubbles should rise to the surface. When mixing resins it is a good idea to leave them a few minutes before pouring, and tap the container gently to remove air bubbles. Their presence will create tiny gaps in the resin, which will spoil the final appearance.

Equipment

No specialist equipment is required, but it is useful to have a good collection of small plastic containers (the caps from aerosol cans will do very nicely), some stirring sticks, and plenty of old newspapers and rags for cleaning up afterwards.

Do not use kitchen utensils such as teaspoons, skewers and so on, unless you have no intention of using them for anything else afterwards! The resin is very tenacious and is almost impossible to remove from surfaces once it has set, so take care.

Finishing

Resin which has set firmly will polish up beautifully with fine sandpaper. Use the finest grade you can – the finer the grit, the better the polish, with 1,000 grit being the minimum to get a reasonable finish. Wet-and-dry can also be used, dry. Metal polish can give an added sheen, but should only be used on the darkest of timbers, as it will tend to discolour lighter wood.

Any of the usual wood finishes can be applied on top of resin once it has dried. Sanding sealer, melamine, Danish oil and wax, for example, are all compatible.

As with all new techniques, it is always a good idea to experiment with scrap pieces first. This is especially important with resins – they can be somewhat unpredictable until you get used to them.

BANKSIA NUT EMBEDDED WITH GOLD-EFFECT RESIN

The starting point for this project is a bud-vase turned from a banksia nut (see Fig 12.1). The vase is 100mm (4in) high, with a maximum width of 53mm ($2\frac{1}{16}$in). The nut was glued to a wooden faceplate prior to turning. Leave the vase attached to the chuck for the following procedures, since it will need to be remounted on the lathe.

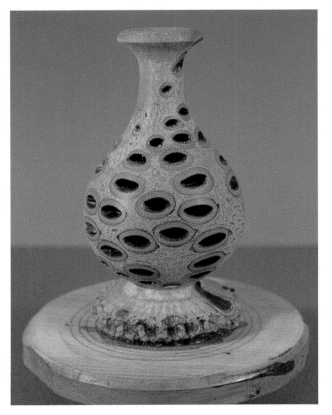

FIG 12.1
Starting point: a bud-vase turned from a banksia nut.

MATERIALS AND METHOD

Plaster of Paris or other suitable filler (optional)

Polyester casting resin and hardener

Brass filler

1   This step is optional, but saves on the quantity of resin required. Mix up a small amount of plaster of Paris, wood filler or any other suitable filling. Push this into the holes in the banksia nut, but make sure that there is still a reasonable gap left below the surface, into which the resin can be pushed (see Fig 12.2).

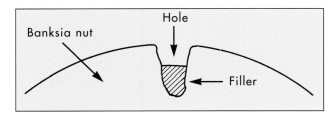

FIG 12.2
Use filler to reduce the depth of the holes in the banksia nut and save on the quantity of resin required.

The layer of resin need only be about 3–4mm ($\frac{1}{8}$in) thick at the surface. With shallow holes, this step can be omitted.

2   Place a measured quantity of resin and brass filler in a small plastic container and mix thoroughly until the correct consistency is obtained. Add hardener, stir, and unless the paste is very thick, tap the container gently to remove air bubbles.

3   Push the mixed resin into some or all of the holes in the banksia nut bud-vase, making sure that the holes are well filled (see Fig 12.3). The number of holes you fill is a matter of personal choice and individual patience. Because the resin may contract slightly, ensure that it remains slightly proud of the surface. Any excess will be sanded away later.

The process of filling the holes can take a long time, depending on the thickness of the paste. If it is fairly runny, it will only be possible to do a few holes at a time, and leave them to set. Otherwise, when you turn the vase round, it will all run out. If the paste is fairly thick, it will be possible to do the whole of one side before leaving the resin to set, as it will tend to stay more or less where you have put it. In either case, you will not be able to fill all the holes in one go, so prepare only a small amount of resin at any one time, unless you have other projects to fill as well.

When all the desired holes have been filled, leave the resin to dry overnight.

4   Remount the vase on the lathe and sand. Since the resin dries very hard, you will need

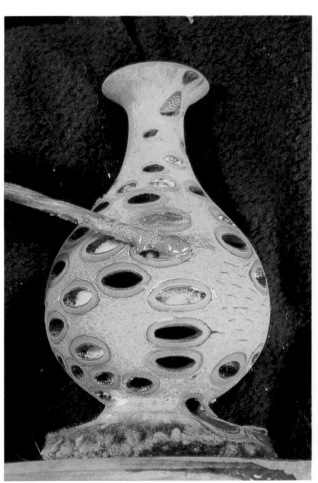

FIG 12.3
Push the mixed resin and brass filler into the holes in the banksia nut.

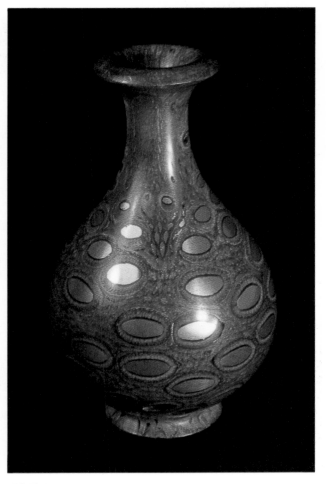

FIG 12.4
The completed vase, sanded and finished.

to use quite a coarse abrasive to begin with. Then gradually work through the grades, finishing with the finest grade you have. *It is essential that some form of respiratory protection is worn at this stage to avoid inhaling the fine resin dust, which could be harmful.*

5   Apply a coat of melamine followed by carnauba wax, or any other preferred finish. Part off.

Fig 12.4 shows the finished bud-vase. Fig 12.5 shows a small burr hollow-form, embedded with resin in a similar way. In this example, the resin was pushed into the natural fissures in the surface of the wood. A groove was cut encircling the neck of the vessel, into which resin was also embedded.

FIG 12.5
A burr hollow-form, embedded with resin in a similar way to the bud-vase.

YEW BOWL EMBEDDED WITH BLACK RESIN

In this and the next project, resin has been embedded along the grain line. Yew was deliberately chosen for its pronounced grain pattern, which lends itself very well to this technique. A groove is cut along the grain line, using a glass-engraving cutter attached to a hand-held Minicraft drill. This technique is described in detail in Chapter 2.

The starting point for this project is a yew bowl 20mm ($\frac{3}{4}$in) deep, with a diameter of 148mm ($5\frac{3}{4}$in).

MATERIALS AND METHOD

Polyester casting resin and hardener

Opaque black pigment

1   Decide which grain lines are to be cut. Care should be taken to ensure that the finished effect looks balanced: the aim is to draw attention to and enhance the grain line, without dominating the entire piece, so a little restraint is required. One, two or three cut grain lines is quite sufficient.

2   Using the Minicraft drill with glass-engraving cutter attached, cut slowly and carefully along a chosen grain line – a steady hand is required (see Fig 12.6).

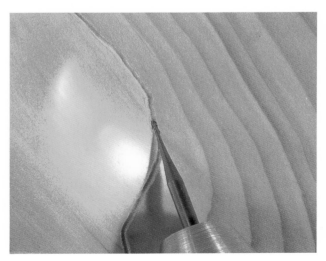

FIG 12.6
Cut along the chosen grain line, using a glass-engraving cutter.

Remember that this grain line continues along the underside of the bowl as well, so follow it right the way round until you arrive back where you started. Fig 12.7 shows the groove cut on the underside of the bowl.

FIG 12.7
The completed groove, cut on the underside of the bowl.

3   Mix up a small quantity of resin and add a tiny amount of opaque black pigment. Mix thoroughly and add the hardener. Stir, and then tap the container gently to remove the air bubbles.

4   Gently run the resin into the groove on one side of the bowl. The resin can be applied using a small stick or similar implement. The bowl was deliberately turned in a fairly shallow shape so that the resin would lie reasonably flat in the groove. With a steep-sided vessel, the resin would have run down the sides.

TIP

Do not apply the resin immediately after adding the hardener. Leave it a few minutes until it gets a little thicker. If a very runny mixture is applied to the groove, the wood fibres will tend to draw the resin up a little by capillary action, and the result will be a grey, smudged appearance in places around the edges of the line. With a thicker mixture, this does not happen.

5   When the resin is dry, repeat with the other side of the bowl, making sure that the edges of the line meet up. Leave to dry (see Fig 12.8).

FIG 12.8
Inlay black resin into the groove and leave to dry.

6   Repeat this procedure with further grain lines if desired.

7   Return the bowl to the lathe and sand, so that the surface is completely smooth. Progress through the grades, finishing with 1,000 grit or finer. *It is essential that some form of respiratory protection is worn at this stage to avoid inhaling the fine resin dust, which could be harmful.*

8   Finish with sanding sealer, melamine or any preferred finish.

Fig 12.9 shows the finished bowl.

FIG 12.9
The finished bowl, seen this time from the top, with two grain lines embedded with resin.

YEW BOWL EMBEDDED WITH SILVER- AND GOLD-EFFECT RESINS

The starting point for this project is a yew bowl 30mm ($1\frac{1}{4}$in) deep, with a diameter of 143mm ($5\frac{5}{8}$in). As in the previous project, the intention here is to embed resin along the grain line, but this time using metallic resin instead of black. Because metal fillers render the resin much thicker, the bowl could be turned with slightly deeper sides, as the resin will be less likely to run out of the grooves.

MATERIALS AND METHOD

Polyester casting resin and hardener

Aluminium filler

Brass filler

1   Decide which grain lines are to be cut, to create a balanced effect. One, two or three will be sufficient.

2   Using the drill and glass-engraver cutter as for the previous project, cut the required grooves, matching up the lines on both sides of the bowl.

3   Mix up two small quantities of resin, one with aluminium filler and the other with brass filler. Add hardener in the usual way and apply the resin to the grooves. Being fairly thick, the

FIG 12.10
Coax the mixed resin into the grooves using a small stick.

resin will need to be coaxed into the grooves using a small stick (see Fig 12.10). In this example, two grooves were filled with brass-powder resin and the third with aluminium-powder resin.

4   When resin has been applied to both sides of the bowl, leave to dry overnight.

5   Return the bowl to the lathe and sand in the usual way, finishing with as fine a grade of sandpaper as you can get. *It is essential that some form of respiratory protection is worn at this stage to avoid inhaling the fine resin dust, which could be harmful.*

6   Apply sanding sealer and wax, or any preferred finish.

Fig 12.11 shows the finished bowl.

FIG 12.11
The finished bowl, showing two grooves filled with brass-powder resin and one with aluminium.

PADAUK BOX DECORATED WITH IVORY-COLOURED RESIN

The starting point for this project is a lidded padauk box 60mm ($2\frac{3}{8}$in) high, with a diameter of 115mm ($4\frac{1}{2}$in). It is still attached to the lathe (see Fig 12.12).

At this stage the lid is tightly attached to the box body. A decorative dovetail recess is cut in the base for later remounting on the lathe, using an expanding dovetail collet chuck. A small recess is turned in the centre of the lid, to receive a finial later.

For added effect, the box is to be inlaid with brass wire and brass tubing prior to adding the resin. This is not absolutely necessary, and the procedure for adding the resin could easily be carried out without the wire or tubing in place.

If you wish to include the wire and tubing, refer to Chapters 1 and 2 for details.

FIG 12.14
Embed the brass tubing and wire, gluing the wire around the inner and outer edges of the wide groove.

FIG 12.12
Starting point: a padauk box with lid.

FIG 12.15
Drill a hole in the top of the turned finial.

FIG 12.13
Cut a wide circular groove in the surface of the box lid.

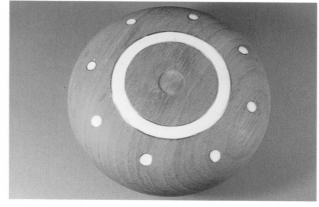

FIG 12.16
Fill the gaps within the brass tubing and wire inlays with mixed resin.

MATERIALS AND METHOD

Brass tubing 7mm ($\frac{1}{4}$ in) diameter (optional)

Brass wire 1mm (0.0394in) thick (optional)

Polyester casting resin and hardener

Opaque ivory pigment

1 Using a 7mm ($\frac{1}{4}$ in) drill bit, drill eight equidistant holes in the flat surface of the top of the lid.

2 With the lathe running, cut a circular groove 8mm ($\frac{5}{16}$ in) wide in the surface of the lid, to the correct depth for the brass wire (see Fig 12.13).

3 Embed the brass wire and tubing following the methods given in Chapters 1 and 2. The wire must be glued around the inner and outer edges of the wide groove. Sand (see Fig 12.14).

4 Remove the box from the lathe and turn a small finial for the top of the lid. Drill a 7mm ($\frac{1}{4}$ in) hole in the top (see Fig 12.15).

5 Inlay some 7mm ($\frac{1}{4}$ in) brass tubing in the hole in the finial, and sand.

6 Mix up a small quantity of resin with some opaque ivory pigment. Add the hardener, and pour the mixture into the gaps within the brass tubing and wire inlays (see Fig 12.16). To allow for shrinkage of the resin during drying, make sure that it is just proud of the surface. Because the top of the box lid is fairly flat, the resin should settle in without any problems of overspill. Leave to dry overnight.

7 Remount the box on the lathe and sand thoroughly, finishing with as fine a grade of sandpaper as possible. *It is essential that some form of respiratory protection is worn at this stage to avoid inhaling the fine resin dust, which could be harmful.*

8 Apply any preferred finish. In this case, sanding sealer and carnauba wax were used. Finally, glue the finial into the centre of the lid.

Fig 12.17 shows the finished box.

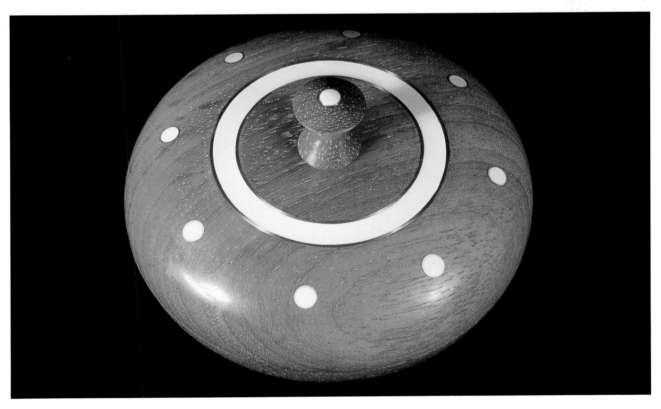

FIG 12.17
The finished box, complete with decorative finial.

13

SCORCHING TECHNIQUES

◆ Safety ◆ Pyrography ◆ Using a gas torch ◆

PROJECTS

◆ Cheeseboard decorated with pyrography ◆ Large beaded and scorched bowl ◆
◆ Sycamore bowl with decorated scorched rim ◆

ESSENTIAL EQUIPMENT

Pyrography tool
Small gas torch
Basic turning tools and materials

RECOMMENDED EQUIPMENT

Carving tool
Minicraft drill

Scorching can be a very effective method of decorating woodturned items – it can also be a lot of fun! This chapter explores two basic techniques: the first is pyrography, which is a well-established technique for decorating a wide variety of wooden items, while the second involves the use of a gas torch for scorching larger areas.

Scorching works on the principle that charred wood is turned a permanent dark brown-black colour. The charring only extends about 1mm ($\frac{1}{32}$ in) or so below the surface, and this fact can be exploited by carving patterns through the charred layer to reveal the paler wood beneath. This technique is illustrated in the final project in this chapter.

SAFETY

Since timber is highly combustible, care must be taken at all times to avoid fires in the workshop. With a pyrography tool this is less of a hazard, because the heat is confined to the point of the tool. With a gas torch, however, a naked flame is used, so the procedure *must be carried out away from flammable chemicals and sawdust or wood shavings*. Always have a bucket of water or a fire extinguisher to hand, just in case. It is inadvisable to use naked flame on timbers which have a high resin content, because of their combustibility.

PYROGRAPHY

Pyrography means, literally, fire-writing. It involves burning a design into the surface of the wood – other materials, such as leather and cork, can also be decorated in this way. A heated tool with a fine point is required, preferably one with a built-in thermostat. Several different types can be used for this technique, but they all work on the same principle.

The first is basically a type of soldering iron, with a tip that is heated by an electrical element. The second consists of an electrically heated hot wire, which is bent into a specific shape. The third, and most common, form of pyrography tool is the type which has an external element close to the tip. Most models are designed to take a variety of interchangeable tips to produce different effects.

Some pyrography tools work off mains voltage, others come with transformers. Fig 13.1 shows a typical design.

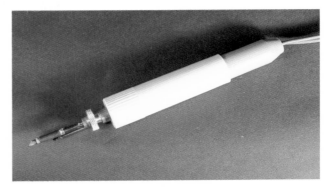

FIG 13.1
A pyrography tool.

SELECTION OF TIMBER

All timber will char, so this technique can be applied to any wood. However, some are more suitable than others, and the following factors should be taken into consideration.

Colour It goes without saying that the paler the wood, the greater will be the contrast between the charred and uncharred areas. Therefore, it is best to avoid dark timbers.

Grain features Pyrography is shown at its best on plain, featureless timbers such as lime, sycamore, box, holly and hornbeam. Where grain figure occurs, it can detract from the effect of the pyrography, so this should be borne in mind. Timbers with pronounced grain *can* be used, but the visual impact of the pyrographic effect will be less pronounced.

Hardness In general, hard close-grained timbers are best for pyrography. Try to avoid timbers which have areas of hard and soft wood, as this causes uneven burning and spoils the effect.

PREPARING THE SURFACE

It is important to ensure that the surface to be decorated has been sanded meticulously – failure to do so will result in uneven definition of the lines. Sealing and polishing take place after the pyrography is complete.

USING THE PYROGRAPHY TOOL

Because the tool is light, with a fine tip, using it is very much like using a pencil. However, unlike a pencil, increased pressure will not produce a darker line. In fact, the pressure should be kept constant at all times. Darker lines will be produced by either increasing the temperature (by adjusting the thermostat) or by moving the tip across the wood more slowly.

Because of the fineness of some of the tips, extremely thin lines can be produced. This makes the tool very versatile for a wide variety of designs, even those with extremely fine lines. In addition to continuous lines, other marks, such as dots, can be made. These can be useful to provide 'shading' and give the effect of depth.

TRANSFERRING THE DESIGN ON TO WOOD

Before starting work with the pyrography tool, you will need to draw the design on to the surface of the wood. There are a number of ways in which this can be done. It can be drawn freehand with a pencil, or copied from a book. It can be traced on to tracing paper, and the paper then placed face-down on the surface of the wood and rubbed to transfer the design. Even transfers and rubber stamps can be used. A little ingenuity is all that is required. If you have no confidence in your own drawing ability, and can find no suitable designs to copy or trace, you can always ask someone else to draw the design for you, but this should rarely be necessary.

ADDING COLOUR

Some pyrographic artists colour the designs after scorching, using stains, inks, water colours and so on. This is purely a matter of personal taste, and may often depend on the nature of the design and the type of object being decorated. If you would like to apply colour, refer to Chapter 5, Dyes and Stains.

PRACTICE

As in all things, practice makes perfect. This is particularly true with pyrography, and it is wise to spend some time practising with the tool on pieces of scrap wood of various densities and colours. After some confidence and proficiency has been gained, you will be in a position to select your first design.

USING A GAS TORCH

A gas torch can be used where larger areas of wood are to be scorched. This is a rather less controlled method of charring, in the sense that it is less localized, and fine lines cannot be produced. Nevertheless, it should not be a completely 'uncontrolled' activity – safety and precision require a degree of control throughout the whole procedure.

Small gas torches which run on butane gas can be purchased from DIY stores and craft shops (see Fig 13.2). These are light and easy to use, and have a relatively small flame which is easy to control. The length of flame is adjustable.

FIG 13.2
A small butane gas torch.

When scorching large areas of wood, progress systematically around the piece, working on one area at a time. However, do *not* allow the flame to rest on any one area for more than a second or two. Keep the flame moving, and if an area is too pale, come back to it when it has had time to cool off, and scorch it a bit more. If the flame is allowed to rest for too long on one spot, more significant burning will occur and the surface will be damaged.

Keep a lookout for thin plumes of smoke coming from one spot. This indicates that slow smouldering is occurring. This must be avoided, because it is hard to detect and will cause deep burning, resulting in patches of charcoal!

> **TIP**
> Keep a damp cloth at your side, and after each small patch has been scorched, blot it with the cloth. This will prevent slow smouldering.

If you are attempting to scorch a surface which has been beaded (see the bowl on page 138), you will find that it is almost impossible to scorch the areas of wood at the very bottom of the beads without over-burning the tops. Consequently, if an even colour is required, you may have to 'cheat' a little by filling the gaps with brown-black dye.

Before scorching, check the surface of the wood for hairline cracks. Although these may be barely visible at this stage, the heat produced during scorching will dry the moisture out of the surface to such an extent that any tiny cracks will open up quite considerably and become visible. This does not always matter, especially if you are keen to achieve an 'antique' look. However, it is worth knowing what to expect.

SCORCHING VERSUS DYEING

Why bother to scorch wood at all – would it not be simpler just to dye it with a brown-black stain?

The first thing to note is that it would not necessarily be simpler. It is not always easy to achieve an even, dark colour using dyes. In addition, you have to choose a finish which is compatible with the chemical base of the dye. With scorching, any finish is suitable, and an even colour is fairly easy to obtain. You may also feel that scorching is a 'cleaner' process than using dyes and stains.

For me, however, the main appeal of scorching lies in the 'textured' effects that it produces – the texture and lustre produced by scorching cannot be reproduced by the use of dyes and stains. Because soft wood burns more readily than harder, denser wood, scorching will tend to differentiate areas of hard and soft wood in a piece. For example, the

less dense spring growth will burn more readily than the denser winter growth, and this results in small ridges appearing on the surface of the wood, highlighting the growth rings. This gives an almost 'antique' effect, not dissimilar to ancient wooden furniture which has been worn into smooth ridges with wear. This effect will vary considerably from one timber to another, being less apparent on timber without pronounced growth rings (tropical timbers, for example). It will also depend very much on the extent of the scorching. It is, perhaps, this unpredictability which adds to the appeal of the technique.

DESIGN CONSIDERATIONS

In the project on page 137, the whole bowl is scorched. It is more usual, however, to scorch only parts of an item, to add interest and to highlight a particular area. It can be particularly effective when applied to the thick rim of a natural-edged bowl, for example.

Where only certain areas are to be scorched, remember that the gas flame cannot produce a sharp line: the surrounding areas will be progressively paler as they get further away from the heat source. Consequently, it is usual to demarcate the edges afterwards and make them more pronounced by returning the item to the lathe and cutting away a thin layer of wood on either side of the area which you wish to remain black. The natural colour of the wood will be revealed, creating clear, sharp lines at the edges of the scorched areas.

FURTHER DECORATION OF SCORCHED AREAS

Rather than simply leaving an area a plain dark colour all over, a whole variety of techniques can be used to cut away segments of the surface to reveal the pale wood below, thus creating patterns. Scoring, carving and drilling are some of the many techniques which can be used, and these are illustrated in the project on page 139. With a little imagination, a whole host of different effects can be created. The surface can be hammered, cut with a Stanley knife, gouged with any variety of carving tools, drilled with different-sized drill bits, and so on. A set of napkin rings or knife handles could be decorated in this way, for example, each being slightly different, yet clearly part of the same set.

CHEESEBOARD DECORATED WITH PYROGRAPHY

The starting point for this project is a cheeseboard surround 248mm (9¾in) in diameter and 15mm (⅝in) deep. The recess for the marble disc is 152mm (6in) in diameter and 7mm (¼in) deep (see Fig 13.3). The surface is finely sanded, but no finish has yet been applied.

The pine used in the illustrated example was not ideal as it had a visible grain pattern, and a plainer timber is recommended. Despite this, the final results proved to be satisfactory.

MATERIALS AND METHOD

Flexible adhesive (e.g. silicone sealant)

Marble disc

1   Draw your design on to the wood using a soft pencil.

2   Plug in the pyrography tool and wait for it to heat up. Test it out on a piece of scrap wood the same as that used for the main item, and make any necessary adjustments to the temperature.

3   Trace gently over the pencil lines with the point of the pyrography tool, adjusting the speed of movement as you go to create the desired effect (see Fig 13.4).

4   Continue in this way over the whole piece, until the design is complete. Some areas may need a little 'touching up', but try to keep this to a minimum.

5   Sand the surface *gently* using very fine sandpaper. Apply the desired finish, and polish.

6   Glue the marble centre in place using a flexible adhesive, such as silicone sealant.

Fig 13.5 shows the finished piece, while Fig 13.6 shows the design in detail.

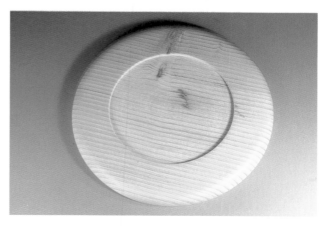

FIG 13.3
Starting point: a cheeseboard surround with a recess ready to receive a marble disc.

FIG 13.4
Etch over the drawn lines with the point of the pyrography tool.

FIG 13.5
The finished cheeseboard, complete with pyrography design and marble disc.

FIG 13.6
The design in detail.

LARGE BEADED AND SCORCHED BOWL

The starting point for this project is a part-turned bowl in European tulipwood. It is 247mm (9¾in) in diameter and 50mm (2in) deep. As can be seen in Fig 13.7, the entire surface of the underside has been beaded, and decorative beading has been added inside the dovetail recess in the centre to match the rest of the piece. The inside will be beaded in the same way. The surface has been finely sanded, but no finish has been applied.

MATERIALS AND METHOD

Brown-black dye

1   With the lathe stationary, light the gas torch and begin to scorch the surface carefully and systematically, keeping the flame moving at all times (see Fig 13.8).

2   Continue in this way, until the entire surface has been satisfactorily scorched. It may be necessary to return to a few patches to

FIG 13.7
Starting point: a part-turned tulipwood bowl, with decorative beading.

re-scorch them if there are areas of unevenness. There will be paler rings caused by the inability of the flame to reach the bottom of the grooves on either side of the beads. Darken these using brown-black dye applied with a fine paintbrush.

137

3　With the lathe running, cut back the surface lightly using 0000 wire wool. Apply sanding sealer and carnauba wax. This gives a rich sheen to the scorched surface which is very pleasing.

4　Reverse-chuck the bowl on to an expanding dovetail collet chuck, and turn the inside. Add beading to match the underside.

5　Scorch the inside of the bowl in the same way as the outside. Fig 13.9 shows the scorched interior of the bowl. The paler rings are visible and will be dyed as before. Cut back using 0000 wire wool, and apply finish as before.

Fig 13.10 shows the finished bowl.

FIG 13.8
Begin to scorch the surface, keeping the flame moving at all times.

FIG 13.9
The scorched interior of the bowl.

FIG 13.10
The finished bowl, with the paler rings dyed brown-black to blend with the scorching.

SYCAMORE BOWL WITH DECORATED SCORCHED RIM

The starting point for this project is a sycamore bowl 260mm (10$\frac{3}{16}$in) in diameter and 42mm (1$\frac{5}{8}$in) deep. The rim is 45mm (1$\frac{3}{4}$in) wide (see Fig 13.11). The rim is scorched using the same technique as in the previous project, and the edges have been sharpened up on the lathe using turning tools to delineate them. In addition, the rim has been scored in concentric circles in one area. This effect was achieved with the lathe running, using the point of a parting tool to cut through the scorched layer into the pale wood underneath. The following stages describe two ways in which the rim can be decorated further.

METHOD

1   Using a Minicraft hand-held drill with a 2mm ($\frac{1}{16}$in) drill bit, drill a series of shallow holes at random within one band of the rim (see Fig 13.12). Continue all the way round the rim.

2   Using a carving tool (in this example, a no. 9, 3mm/$\frac{1}{8}$in) gouge a series of lines around the edge of the rim, each approximately 9mm ($\frac{3}{8}$in) long (see Fig 13.13). The lines do not need to be carved accurately; in this example, they were gouged out fairly quickly freehand, with no pencil lines to mark the position. This technique has created a 'primitive' effect which is rather pleasing.

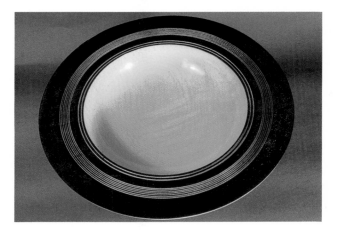

FIG 13.11
Starting point: a sycamore bowl with scorched rim.

FIG 13.12
Drill shallow holes randomly within one band of the bowl rim.

Fig 13.14 shows the finished bowl. Fig 13.15 shows the underside, which has scorched detail to tie in with the design on the upper surface.

FIG 13.13
Gouge lines around the edge of the rim, using a carving tool.

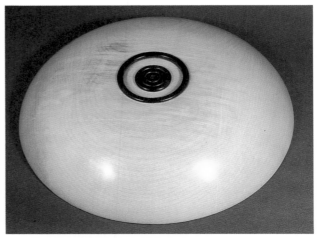

FIG 13.15
The underside of the finished piece.

FIG 13.14
The finished bowl, with scorched detail on the underside to tie in with the design on the upper surface.

14
ALTERING SURFACE
TEXTURE

◆ Planning ◆ Techniques ◆ 'Dimples' and 'pimples' ◆

PROJECTS

◆ Pewter-effect bowl with 'dimpled' rim ◆ Sycamore bowl with 'pimpled' rim ◆

ESSENTIAL EQUIPMENT

Device for punching wood, e.g. centre punch
Steam bath
Basic turning tools and materials

Texture is one of the most appealing aspects of wood. The tactile quality of woodturned items is an important part of their appeal: at craft fairs, exhibitions and galleries, the first thing people want to do on seeing a turned bowl, vase or other item is to pick it up and feel it. Glassware, ceramics and metal do not have this tactile quality – it is unique to wood.

However, it is not just the 'feel' of texture which is appealing: texture also affects the appearance of the surface. Tiny troughs and hollows cast shadows, which can sometimes make the surface more 'interesting', and consequently many turners use specific techniques to alter subtly the texture of given items.

PLANNING

Before setting about your favourite bowl with hammers, chisels, punches and other tools designed to mark the surface in some way, it is advisable to give a bit of thought to the effect you would like to create. As with most decorative techniques, although good effects *can* be created almost at random, the best results are often produced with a specific aim in mind. Ask yourself the following questions:

- Do I want to alter the surface texture of this particular piece at all? The answer may well be 'No'. It could be that this particular item is sufficiently interesting and attractive without doing any more to it, in which case, leave it alone.

- Why do I want to alter the surface texture? Maybe you find the piece a little 'dull', but before deciding to work on the surface texture, it might be worth considering whether a different decorative technique such as some form of inlay, or colouring, might be more appropriate.

- Am I going to alter the texture of the entire surface? There are no rules here – it is entirely up to you. Remember, though, that contrast is an important feature, and sometimes a better effect can be gained by *selective* texturing. In other words, by texturing just *some* of the surface and leaving the rest smooth, the visual

impact might be greater than if the whole surface were textured.

- Exactly where should the texture be applied? Again, this is a matter of personal taste, but it could be that certain areas could usefully be highlighted, such as a rim, a foot, or perhaps the widest part of a curve.

- Which texturing method should I use? This will depend partly on the tools and equipment you have available, but will be determined more by the visual effect you want to achieve. You may, for example, wish to produce a soft, subtle effect, or strong, sharp lines, or create a pattern of dots and curves. You may wish to highlight the grain, produce a regular pattern on a box lid, create alternating rough and smooth areas, and so on. Choose the technique which best suits your purposes.

TECHNIQUES

You are probably already familiar with a variety of methods of creating 'texture' on the surface of wooden items. Some techniques need special equipment, but most require only ingenuity. Those described below are just a few of the possibilities, so do experiment and devise your own texturing techniques.

SANDBLASTING

Some beautiful effects can be produced by sandblasting. It is a technique which is best used on soft wood, where there is a pronounced pattern of growth rings, and works on the principle that the soft spring growth is more readily worn away than the harder winter growth. In this way, a series of ridges are formed, which follow the pattern of the growth rings.

Unfortunately, sandblasting is not a readily accessible technique for most people, since it requires the use of special equipment which sprays fine grit at high velocity, usually by means of a compressor. Protective clothing must be worn and safety precautions observed. For those with access to such equipment, it might be an interesting exploration, and the resulting effects can be extremely pleasing.

CHATTER WORK

It is possible to buy specially made 'chatter tools' for carrying out this technique, although some people use or adapt ordinary woodturning tools, files and so on to produce the same effects. Chatter work is based on the principle that if the tool is supported a long way from the workpiece (by moving back the tool rest), this will exploit and increase the effect of any vibration, producing an intricate spiral effect caused by the vibrating or 'chattering' of the tool against the surface of the wood as it rotates on the lathe. Indeed, we have all unintentionally produced similar spiral effects on our turning from time to time, through accidentally letting the bevel bounce hard against the wood, especially when the tool rest is too far from the work. This principle, when controlled and used deliberately in specific areas, can produce extremely attractive effects.

USING ELECTRIC DRILLS AND ATTACHMENTS

Ordinary hand-held electric drills can be used with a variety of attachments, such as cutters, burrs, small sanding wheels and so on, to good effect. Each attachment will produce a different type of texture when applied to the wood – even ordinary drill bits can be used. The small Minicraft drills are particularly useful for such work since, being light, they are comfortable to hold and can be used with a degree of precision. It is worth experimenting with different attachments on some scrap wood to explore the variety of textural effects which can be achieved.

USING CARVING TOOLS

Carving gouges and chisels come in all shapes and sizes, so there is no limit to the type of groove which can be made using them: small, shallow grooves in a random pattern; regular V-shaped grooves in a circular direction; small, deep, diagonal cuts – the possibilities are endless.

This is probably one of the easiest methods of creating texture. Although some skilful tool use is required to produce regular patterns, very little is needed to create a random effect, although simple safety precautions, such as never cutting towards your fingers, should always be observed. If you are able to gather together a few sharp carving tools, a few hours spent practising – to gain familiarity with the tools and the effects they can create – would be time well spent.

HAMMERING, BEATING AND PUNCHING

Small hammers, nails and punches of all descriptions can also be used to create texture. Provided that care is taken in their use, there is no need to look any further than your workshop for the most commonplace items which can be used successfully to create a textured surface.

'DIMPLES' AND 'PIMPLES'

The two projects in this chapter have been chosen to demonstrate a very simple technique, which can produce two rather different effects.

THE 'DIMPLED' EFFECT

This technique primarily involves the punching of small holes in the surface of the wood to create a 'dimpled' effect. Holes *can* be punched using a hammer and a blunted nail, but I use an automatic centre punch (see Fig 14.1) because it is quick, easy and safe to use, and produces regular-sized holes of equal depth.

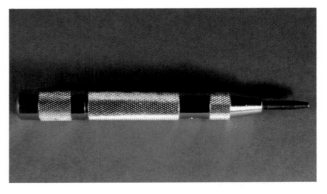

FIG 14.1
An automatic centre punch.

The punch is used by gently pushing the point into the surface of the wood. This action releases a trigger mechanism, which then forces the point into the surface at high speed. The precise depth of penetration can be controlled by a knob at one end of the punch. With soft woods, the penetration depth adjustment can be set at its minimum, because the wood will offer little resistance to the force of the penetrating point; with harder woods, the adjustment may need to be set rather higher.

Using this method, a series of small, shallow holes of identical diameter and depth can be produced with a high degree of accuracy. The shape of the point will determine the shape of the hole. I have found that best results are obtained after the point has been blunted on a grinding wheel. This not only creates a nice 'rounded' hole, but is also less likely to tear the fibres.

The best effects are produced with dense, close-grained timbers. Where a softer wood is used, there is sometimes a tendency for the grain to tear. This is not particularly important when producing a 'dimpled' effect, but for the 'pimpled' effect described below it is more significant.

Because the centre punch is so easy to use with a high degree of precision, regular or irregular patterns can be produced with ease. The holes can be close, spaced apart, in straight lines, circles, curves or what you will.

THE 'PIMPLED' EFFECT

In textural terms, this is rather like 'dimples' in reverse. The effect is one of small, raised bumps on the surface instead of small depressions. The technique for producing the 'pimples' is one of my favourites. This is partly because it is so different and unusual, but mainly because it is simple yet somehow clever – I was told about this method third-hand, but had never seen it done, and despite its simplicity, I would never have thought of it myself.

The procedure is initially the same as for producing 'dimples'. A centre punch is an ideal tool for this technique, because it is essential that all the holes are punched to the same depth – or as near as possible. (In practice, some will always be *fractionally* deeper than others.) After the holes have been punched, return the wood to the lathe and cut back the surface, using any appropriate turning tool, to a depth which corresponds to the depth of the dimples. In other words, cut away the

surface until it is *only just* completely smooth (see Fig 14.2). It is essential to cut away to exactly this depth – no more and no less. I prefer to remove the last fraction with sandpaper. Although the surface should now be completely smooth, the 'dots' caused by the dimples will still be visible, because the compressed wood appears a slightly different colour from the rest.

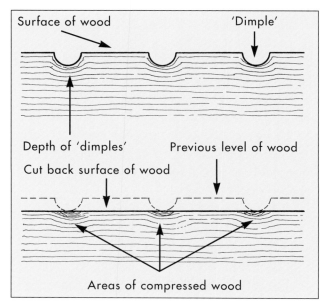

FIG 14.2
Cut back the surface of the wood to a depth corresponding to that of the 'dimples'.

Now remove the workpiece from the lathe and hold it over a steam bath (a roasting tin full of water on top of the stove works satisfactorily). The steam will swell the wood fibres in the 'dots' of compressed wood caused by the punch, and as this happens, the places which were mere dots now, as if by magic, swell into small 'pimples' all over the surface (Fig 14.3). When the swelling is complete – this takes a few minutes – leave the wood to dry and then sand it *very lightly* with 0000 wire wool. A finish can then be applied in the normal way. The textured effect produced by this technique not only looks very attractive but is also extremely tactile. It is advisable to experiment first with samples of different timbers as the final results will be affected by factors such as the density of the wood, whether end grain or side gain is used, and so on.

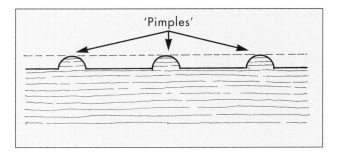

FIG 14.3
The steam causes the areas of compressed wood to swell and form 'pimples' on the surface.

PEWTER-EFFECT BOWL WITH 'DIMPLED' RIM

For this project, only certain sections of the wood surface were textured, to provide a contrast with the remaining smooth areas. The piece was coloured with dye and silver cream in the final stages, but this is, of course, optional.

The starting point for this project is a sycamore bowl 43mm (1¾in) deep, with a diameter of 253mm (10in) and rim width of 60mm (2⅜in). The rim sweeps downwards slightly. Fig 14.4 shows the underside of the bowl, which at this stage is part-turned. Fig 14.5 shows the underside after ebonizing with black dye, and Fig 14.6 the same surface after an application of silver cream. The resulting colour is similar to pewter. Fig 14.7 shows the top of the bowl after turning is complete.

FIG 14.5
The underside of the bowl, now ebonized using black dye.

FIG 14.6
The same surface, after application of silver cream to achieve a 'pewter' effect.

FIG 14.4
Starting point: a sycamore bowl, shown here with the underside part turned.

FIG 14.7
The top of the bowl, with turning complete.

MATERIALS AND METHOD

Black dye (optional)

Silver cream (optional)

1   Using a soft pencil, mark out on the rim the areas which are to be textured. In this example, a scalloped shape was chosen. Using the automatic centre punch, punch a series of randomly spaced holes within the confines of the marked areas. Try to keep the holes fairly evenly spaced (see Fig 14.8). Fig 14.9 shows the rim after all the holes have been punched.

2   Sand carefully, and ebonize the top surface to match the bottom, following the instructions in Chapter 5 (see Fig 14.10).

FIG 14.8
Punch holes randomly within the marked areas, using an automatic centre punch.

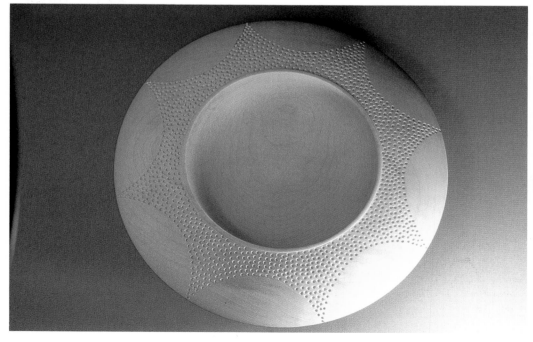

FIG 14.9
All the holes have now been punched on the bowl rim.

3   Apply silver cream to create a 'pewter' effect, and polish with a soft cloth.

Stages 2 and 3 can be omitted, in which case sand lightly with 0000 wire wool and apply sanding sealer or melamine and wax instead.

TIP

If you are intending to use wood dye, especially a water-based type, it may be necessary to 're-punch' the holes lightly after the dye has dried. This is because the moisture in the dye can cause the compressed fibres in the holes to swell slightly and puff out. Re-punching with the centre punch may not be necessary; I have found that simply working the point of the punch gently in a circular fashion in each hole will press the fibres back in place, to create nice clean holes with sharp edges once again.

Fig 14.11 shows the finished bowl.

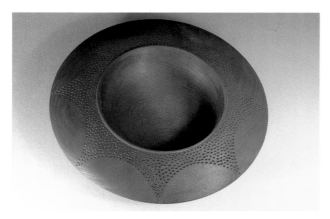

FIG 14.10
The top surface of the bowl after ebonizing.

FIG 14.11
The finished pewter-effect bowl with 'dimpled' rim.

SYCAMORE BOWL WITH 'PIMPLED' RIM

The starting point for this project is a sycamore bowl 43mm ($1\frac{3}{4}$in) deep, with a diameter of 225mm ($8\frac{7}{8}$in) and rim width of 50mm (2in). As in the previous project, the rim is slightly downward sweeping (see Fig 14.12). Although sycamore was used in this example, a harder wood is recommended.

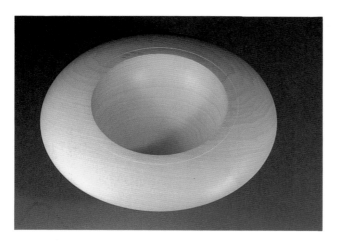

FIG 14.12
Starting point: a sycamore bowl with a slightly downward-sweeping rim, similar to that used in the previous project.

In this example, texture is applied to the whole of the upper side of the rim, except for the narrow raised band around the hollow. A decorative dovetail recess is cut in the base to allow the bowl to be remounted easily on the lathe using an expanding dovetail collet chuck.

METHOD

1   Using an automatic centre punch, punch a series of evenly spaced, random holes all over the bowl rim (see Fig 14.13). Fig 14.14 shows the bowl after all the holes have been punched.

2   Return the bowl to the lathe, and remove the top surface of the rim to a depth equivalent to the depth of the holes. If preferred, the last stages of this can be done by sanding. Sand finely, finishing with 400 grit sandpaper. At this stage the surface will be completely smooth, but 'dots' will be seen on the surface, indicating the areas of compressed wood (see Fig 14.15).

FIG 14.13
Punch evenly spaced holes all over the bowl rim, using an automatic centre punch.

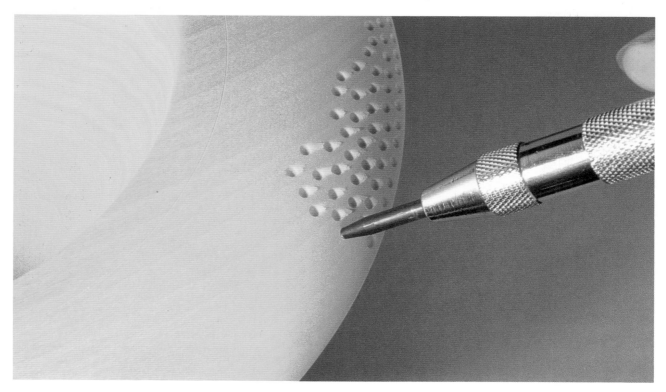

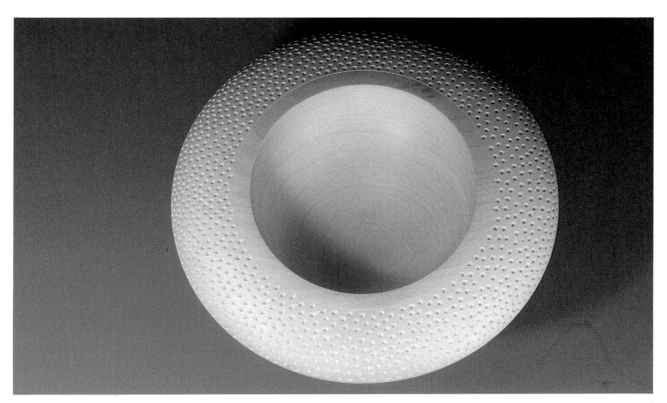

FIG 14.14
All the holes have now been punched.

FIG 14.15
Sand the surface completely smooth – the dots indicate areas of compressed wood.

3   Hold the bowl face-down over a steam bath –
    it is not necessary to allow the wood to come
    in contact with the boiling water. The 'dots'
    will be transformed into raised 'pimples' (see
    Fig 14.16).

4   When the bowl is dry, cut back the raised grain
    lightly with 0000 wire wool. Be careful not to
    be too vigorous at this stage: you do not want
    to 'blunt' the raised areas.

5   Apply sanding sealer and carnauba wax, or any
    other preferred finish.

    Fig 14.17 shows the finished bowl.

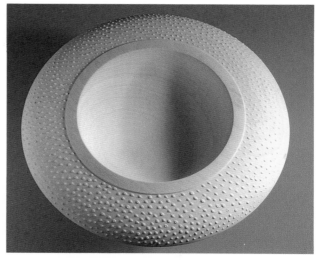

FIG 14.16
The 'pimples' created by holding the bowl over a steam bath.

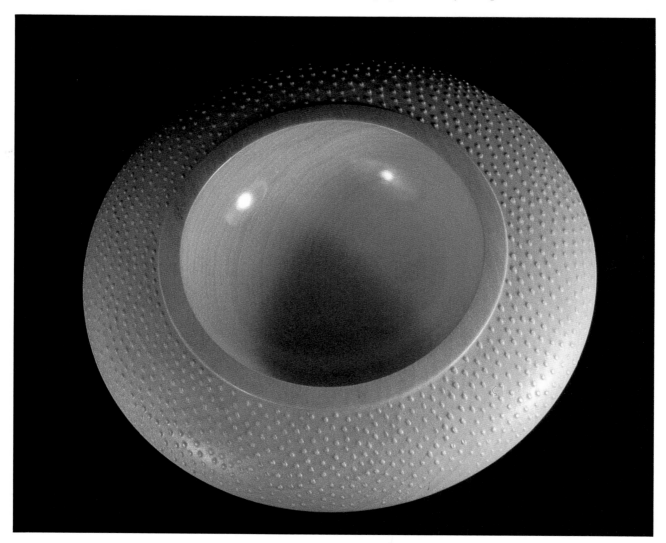

FIG 14.17
The completed bowl, cut back lightly and finished.

15
CARVING

◆ Selection of timber ◆ Tools ◆ Safety ◆ Support methods ◆ Techniques ◆

PROJECTS

◆ Platter with carved fretwork rim ◆ 'Pineapple' box ◆

ESSENTIAL EQUIPMENT

Assorted carving tools
Fretsaw
Mini-hacksaw
Basic turning tools and materials

Carving and turning are skills which complement each other extremely well, and can be combined to create some stunning forms.

It is beyond the scope of this chapter to give details of precise carving techniques, but there are many excellent books and courses on carving available for those wishing to develop the skills properly. My aim here is to present some brief ideas on the ways in which *simple* carving methods can be used to enhance turning. The techniques described do not require a high level of skill, nor a great many tools – all that is needed is a basic understanding of grain direction and how tools cut, and some patience. For those who have never carved before, it would be advisable to practise with some basic carving tools on pieces of scrap wood before embarking on anything special, as there is no substitute for hands-on experience. Having said that, the projects outlined in this chapter have been chosen because they require very few tools and a minimum level of skill, while still producing attractive results.

SELECTION OF TIMBER

It is best to use a fairly soft wood for carving, since this will offer the least resistance to the tool. Lime is one of the most popular woods for carvers, as it is extremely easy to work yet gives a good finish. Being a plain-coloured timber with no marked grain features, it is ideal for showing the carving to its best advantage. Sycamore is another wood which is reasonably easy to carve. Occasionally, however, carvers will deliberately select a bicoloured timber, and use this difference in colour as a feature in some way. Clearly, the choice of timber will depend on the design intentions.

TOOLS

The greater the variety of carving tools you have at your disposal the better, but most people manage with whatever they happen to have. For some cuts – particularly where undercutting is involved – specific tools are required, but for most straightforward cuts just a few basic gouges of different sizes and shapes are all that is needed. In addition to straight and skew chisels, gouges are

available in blade widths ranging from 2mm ($\frac{1}{16}$ in) to 50mm (2in), and a range of curves from very shallow (no. 3) to extremely curved (no. 11).

Rifflers are extremely useful. These are small files in a variety of shapes, some with curves (see Fig 15.1), which are designed for filing or rasping away wood in areas which are not easily accessible to chisels or gouges. Many carvers use mallets during the initial stages of their work, but these are not necessary for the projects outlined in this chapter.

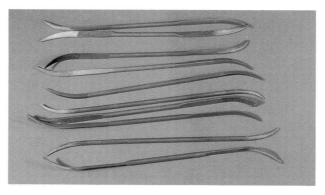

FIG 15.1
A collection of rifflers in various shapes.

Carving tools are not cheap, but they can often be acquired secondhand from market stalls, car boot sales, jumble sales and friends. Start with just a few of the basic shapes and sizes, and buy more specialized tools as and when they are needed. Assorted grades of abrasive will also be required.

> ## TIP
> Emery boards, for manicure purposes, are available from chemists, and these can be very useful for sanding along flat, straight lines or angled surfaces. They are very cheap, and have a coarse side and a finer side.

SAFETY

Compared with woodturning, carving is a relatively safe activity. However, it is remarkably easy to sustain cuts on the hands because the tools must be kept *extremely* sharp at all times. *Never* cut towards your hands: it is very easy for the tool to slip and make a very deep cut.

SUPPORT METHODS

There are various ways in which carvers support the workpiece. Vices are often used, or large screws inserted into the bottom of the block, attached to a frame or support. In the projects outlined in this chapter no special means of support is necessary, since the pieces are not sufficiently large, heavy or awkward to merit this.

TECHNIQUES

This chapter outlines just three of the simplest of the many carving techniques you can try.

CHIP CARVING

This could be considered one of the easiest forms of carving, since it requires only one tool, and simply involves cutting and removing small segments, or 'chips' of wood, to form a picture or pattern. Despite its simplicity, however, the designs produced by this method can be extremely intricate and complex.

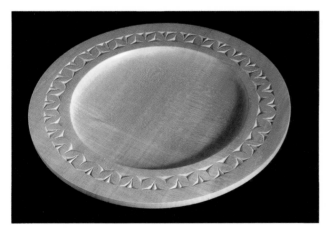

FIG 15.2
A shallow bowl with a chip-carved rim.

Although specially designed chip-carving knives can be purchased, it is possible to cut the designs quite satisfactorily using a *sharp* Stanley knife with a straight blade. Straightforward though the technique may be, it is not necessarily easy to master: there is a certain knack to making good, regular, clean cuts that can only be learned through practice. When the skill has been acquired, it can be a relatively quick method of carving, and very pleasing to accomplish. It is also very versatile, and can be used to decorate a wide variety of items. Fig 15.2 shows a shallow bowl with a chip-carved pattern around the rim; Fig 15.3 shows the 'pattern' for this particular design. For those wishing to develop the skill of chip carving, there are some excellent books available which explain the technique (see Bibliography on page 165).

FRETWORK OR 'PIERCED' CARVING

This technique involves the use of a fretsaw to remove whole sections from thin areas of wood. The remaining sections are then carved. This is a form of carving often seen in churches to decorate screens and panels. The first project in this chapter uses this method to decorate the rim of a platter.

CARVING 'IN THE ROUND'

This is a term used to describe three-dimensional carving, as opposed to flat, two-dimensional work such as 'relief carving', for example. All sides of the piece are carved rather than just one, which may be the case on a panel or frieze. The second project in this chapter uses this technique to transform a plain box into the shape of a pineapple.

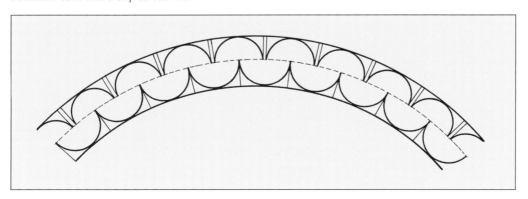

FIG 15.3
The pattern for the chip-carving design shown in Fig 15.2.

PLATTER WITH CARVED FRETWORK RIM

The starting point for this project is a sycamore platter 320mm (12½in) in diameter, with a rim width 50mm (2in) and rim depth of 5.5mm (¼in) (see Fig 15.4). Fretsaw blades are available in a range of widths, but for this type of work a fairly fine blade is needed, in order that it can turn freely around sharp corners. However, it must not be so fine that it keeps breaking. A no. 1 gouge should be satisfactory. If you have an electric fretsaw (or jigsaw) you may prefer to use this, to save time.

MATERIALS AND METHOD

Sandpaper

Soft, colourless polishing wax (e.g. Briwax)

1   Select a suitable design. An important factor to bear in mind is that, because regular segments are to be removed completely from the rim, sufficient wood must remain to give adequate strength. Consequently, try to avoid creating large holes bordered by very fine strands of wood, since this will cause unnecessary fragility.

   If you choose a repeating pattern, you will need to work out an appropriate width for one 'unit', so that a multiple of complete units will fit into the circle. In this example, a single bird was the repeating unit, and 18 birds were fitted into the circular rim. This stage of marking out can take rather a long time, since repeated minor adjustments may need to be made to the size of the unit.

2   Draw the finished design on to the bowl rim, leaving a border at both inner and outer edges of the rim (see Fig 15.5). The outlines of the birds in this example 'overlap' with each border slightly. This not only creates an interesting effect, but also enables the tails and wing tips to be carved finely without causing fragility.

3   During the drilling and sawing stages the work will need to be supported. This is most easily done by keeping the platter attached to the lathe and securing the headstock rigidly at intervals, so that the work is held firmly but can be rotated as necessary. Drill a hole in each segment which is to be cut away (see Fig 15.6).

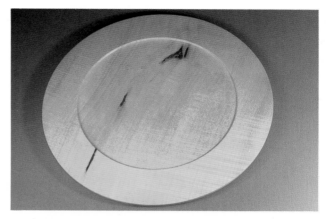

FIG 15.4
Starting point: a sycamore platter, ready for carving.

FIG 15.5

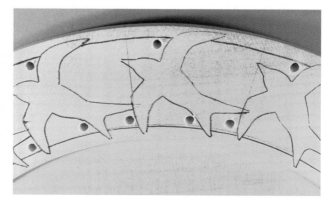

FIG 15.6
Drill a hole in each segment that is to be cut away.

4   Loosen one of the wing nuts on the U-frame of the fretsaw to remove one end of the blade. Thread this end through one of the holes and reconnect it to the U-frame. Apply tension to the blade and retighten the wing nut.

5   Begin to saw along the marked lines (see Fig 15.7).

6   Repeat steps 4 and 5 until all of the segments have been removed (see Fig 15.8).

7   Using a carving gouge, carve away all the square edges of each bird (see Fig 15.9). A 5mm ($\frac{3}{16}$in) no. 2 carving gouge was used in this example, although a close approximation to this would be satisfactory. In the same way,

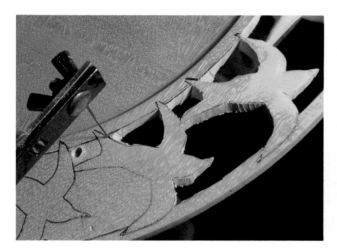

FIG 15.7
Begin to saw along the marked lines, using a fretsaw.

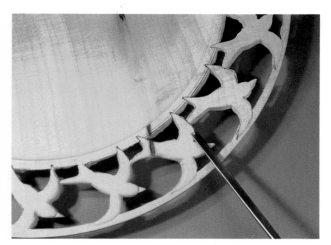

FIG 15.9
Carve away the square edges, using a carving gouge.

TIP

If the fretsaw blade keeps breaking, it could be because you are trying to go too fast and are pressing too hard. Do not press: allow the blade to slide gently over the wood. If you find that the blade *still* breaks, try a slightly thicker one.

carve away the square edges of the borders on the sides facing in towards the centre of the rim. All edges should now be rounded. Remember to carve the underside of the rim as well as the top!

8   File away the rough edges using a curved riffler (see Fig 15.10).

FIG 15.8
All the segments have now been cut away.

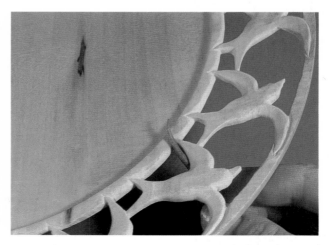

FIG 15.10
File away all rough edges, using a curved riffler.

9   Sand, using successively finer grades of abrasive until all surfaces are completely smooth, finishing with 400 grit.

10   Apply sanding sealer and cut back with 0000 wire wool. Apply a suitable colourless polish.

Fig 15.11 shows the finished platter. Fig 15.12 shows the underside. Note the (optional) carved bird inset into the recess, to match the design on the rim.

FIGS 15.11 AND 15.12
The finished platter, with a carved bird inset into the recess on the underside.

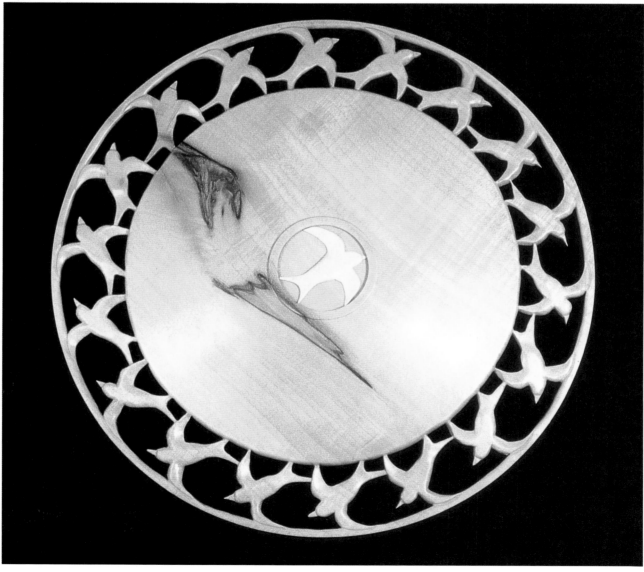

'PINEAPPLE' BOX

The starting point for this project is a turned lime box which has been shaped to resemble the form of a pineapple (see Fig 15.13). It is 135mm (5$\frac{5}{16}$in) long (high) excluding the base, and 100mm (4in) in diameter.

The box is still attached to the remains of the blank at both ends. The point at which the lid joins the body of the box occurs about one-third of the way down from the 'top', i.e. one-third of the distance from the headstock end. A small base has been turned at the tailstock end, and the headstock end will be parted off when marking out is complete. The walls of the box must be fairly thick (approximately 12mm/$\frac{1}{2}$in) to allow for the depth of the carving. At this stage the lid is very tightly fitting, and (hopefully!) will remain so until carving is complete.

Although the box is not truly spherical, for the sake of convenience and clarity I have likened it to a globe in the instructions below, and have chosen to use corresponding terminology.

MATERIALS AND METHOD

Red and black pens

1   Using a pencil, mark out lines of 'longitude' all the way round the circumference (see Fig 15.14).

These lines should be equidistant, and the distance apart will be determined partly by the desired size of the pineapple 'segments'. Determining the correct distance (and hence the number of lines) is not easy, and is achieved largely through trial and error. In this particular example, the lines were spaced at a distance of approximately 15mm ($\frac{5}{8}$in) there being 24 lines altogether.

2   Mark out the lines of 'latitude' (see Fig 15.15). Again, these need to be carefully spaced at regular intervals, but in this case, they are *not* all the same distance apart, being closer towards the 'poles'. This is because the segments on a real pineapple become smaller towards each end. The lines of 'longitude' become correspondingly closer towards the poles, so the squares formed by the

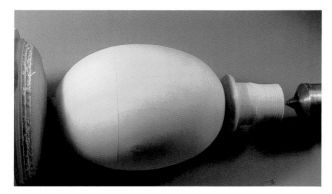

FIG 15.13
Starting point: a lidded lime box, turned to resemble the shape of a pineapple.

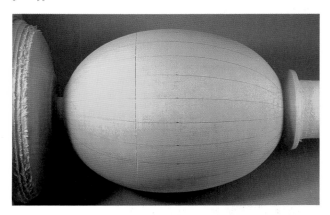

FIG 15.14
Mark out lines of 'longitude' on the surface of the box.

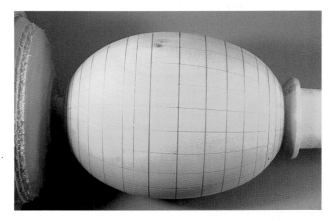

FIG 15.15
Mark out lines of 'latitude'.

intersections of the lines of longitude and latitude are biggest around the 'equator' and smallest at the 'poles'. The segments thus created will be *approximately* square. In this example there are 18 lines of 'latitude', the ones at either end being very narrow.

157

3   Join up all the diagonals in one direction, using alternating lines of black and red (see Fig 15.16).

4   Repeat step 3 with the diagonals in the other direction. Fig 15.17 (a–f) shows a diagramatic sequence of the above stages.

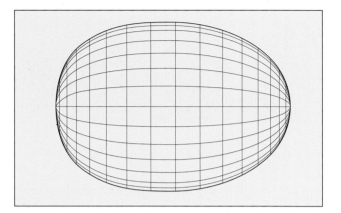

a) Lines of latitude and longitude.

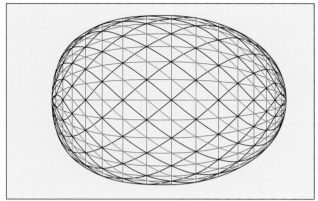

d) Red diagonals drawn in between the first set.

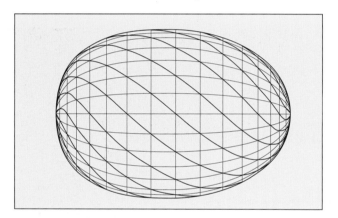

b) First set of diagonals in black.

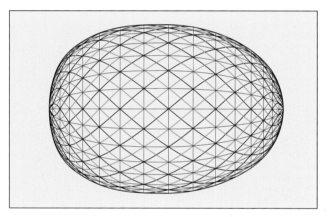

e) Red diagonals (in opposite direction) drawn in between the second set.

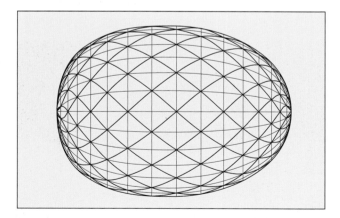

c) Second set of diagonals (in opposite direction), in black.

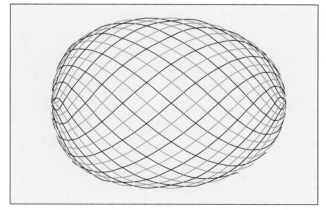

f) Diagonals complete. (Lines of latitude and longitude erased, for clarity.)

FIG 15.17 (a–f)
The sequence of drawings above illustrate one method of marking out. In the example shown, all the black diagonals have been drawn first, and the red diagonals inserted afterwards.

5   Using a mini-hacksaw, saw carefully along all the black diagonal lines to a depth of approximately 2–3mm ($\frac{1}{8}$in) (see Fig 15.18). Part off from the lathe.

TIP

It is useful to make a 'depth-stop' on the hacksaw blade by fixing a straight strip of metal to it 1–2mm ($\frac{1}{32}$–$\frac{1}{16}$in) away from the edge of the blade. This will prevent the blade cutting too deeply and will ensure that all the cuts are made to the same depth (see Fig 15.19).

6   Using a 12mm ($\frac{1}{2}$in) no. 3 carving gouge (or similar), carve from the red lines down towards the bottom of the grooves on the black lines (see Fig 15.20). Do not cut away any wood from the red lines themselves, which should still be visible (see Fig 15.21). The result will be curving spiral slopes all in one direction (see Fig 15.22).

7   Starting from the same red diagonal lines, carve down towards the black lines on the other side. This will result in a series of spiral ridges and troughs all following the same direction (see Figs 15.23 and 15.24).

8   At regular intervals along each ridge, there will be saw marks from the remains of the cuts you made along the black lines (see Fig 15.22). These are the lines along which further 'troughs' are to be cut. Each saw line should be

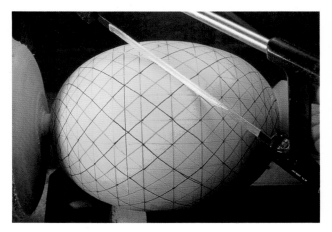

FIG 15.16
Join up the diagonals, using alternative lines of black and red.

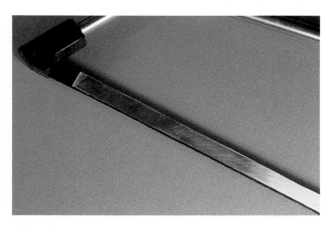

FIG 15.19
A straight strip of metal attached to the blade of a hacksaw as a 'depth-stop'.

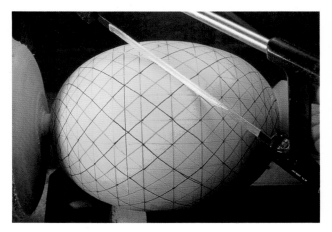

FIG 15.18
Saw along the black diagonal lines to a depth of approximately 2–3mm ($\frac{1}{16}$ – $\frac{1}{8}$ in).

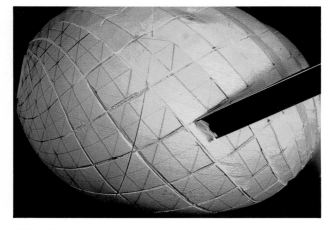

FIG 15.20
Cut from the red lines down to the bottom of the cut grooves on the black lines.

159

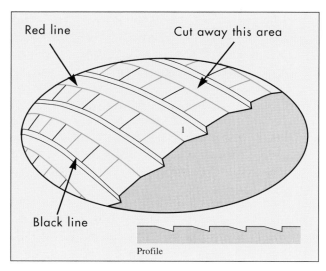

FIG 15.21
Do not cut away any wood from the red lines, which should still be visible.

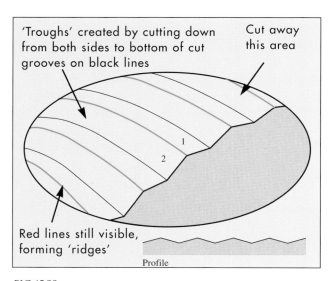

FIG 15.23
The result of the second round of cuts is a series of spiral 'ridges' and 'troughs'.

FIG 15.22
The result of the first round of cuts is a series of curving spiral slopes, all in one direction.

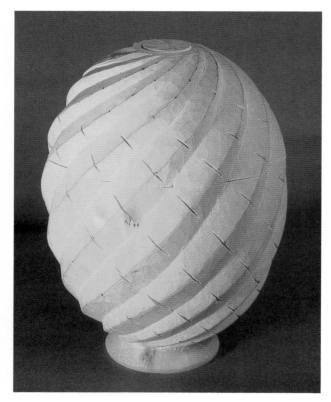

FIG 15.24
The 'ridges' and 'troughs' can clearly be seen on the workpiece.

continuous. If it is not, this means that you have cut slightly deeper with the gouge than the original grooves which were cut with the hacksaw. If this is the case, use the mini-

hacksaw once more to extend the cuts, so that they join up to form continuous lines.

9   Repeat steps 6 and 7, but in the direction of the *other* diagonal lines, so that similar ridges

and troughs will be created at right angles to the previous ones. Because by now most of the marked lines will have been cut away, it will make things easier if you mark a series of adjacent diagonal crosses along each ridge in pencil, the centre of each cross occurring at the peak of each ridge. Starting at the centre of each cross, cut downwards as before, towards the bottom of each groove (see Fig 15.25). Effectively, you are once again cutting from red diagonals to black diagonals, except that this may not be so apparent this time because most of the markings will have been cut away (see Fig 15.26). Continue to cut until you have completed all the sloping cuts in one direction.

10 Repeat, this time cutting down towards the grooves on the other side (see Fig 15.27). It is at this stage that the characteristic 'segments' of the pineapple begin to emerge, and all the effort appears worthwhile at last! Fig 15.28 shows a plan grid of the procedure.

11 Sand gently, taking care not to blunt the edges of the 'pyramids', and finish with sanding sealer and wax, or any preferred finish.

12 Now make the 'leaves'. Experienced carvers may wish to carve realistic leaves. For those who, like myself, lack this level of carving skill, the following guidelines will produce stylized leaves which, while botanically less than

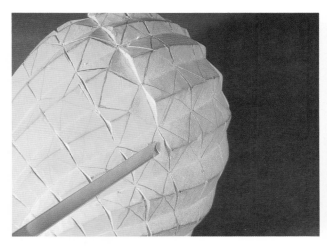

FIG 15.25
Cut downwards towards the bottom of each groove.

FIG 15.27
The 4th round of cuts reveals the completed 'pyramids'.

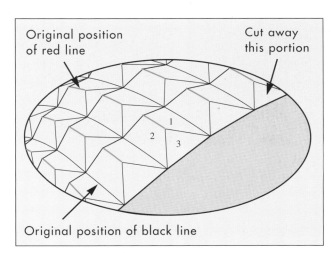

FIG 15.26
Cut again from the original positions of the red lines to those of the black lines, as shown.

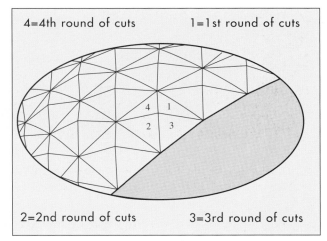

FIG 15.28
A plan grid of the cutting procedure.

accurate, are nevertheless recognizable, and reasonably easy to carve! First, turn the shape shown in Fig 15.29.

13 Mark a five-pointed star on the top of each 'disc' (see Fig 15.30). The points on the top

star should be misaligned with those on the bottom star.

14 Cut along the lines using a mini-hacksaw and part off the leaf structure (see Fig 15.31). The resulting form is shown in Fig 15.32.

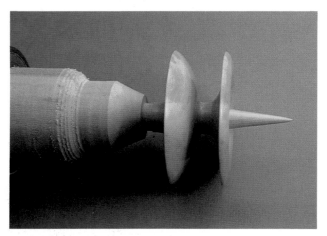

FIG 15.29
Turn the shape for the beginning of the leaf structure.

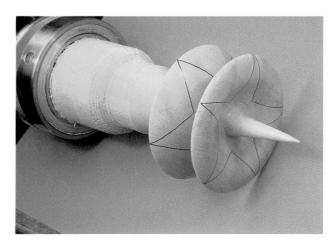

FIG 15.30
Mark a five-pointed star on the top of each disc, with the points

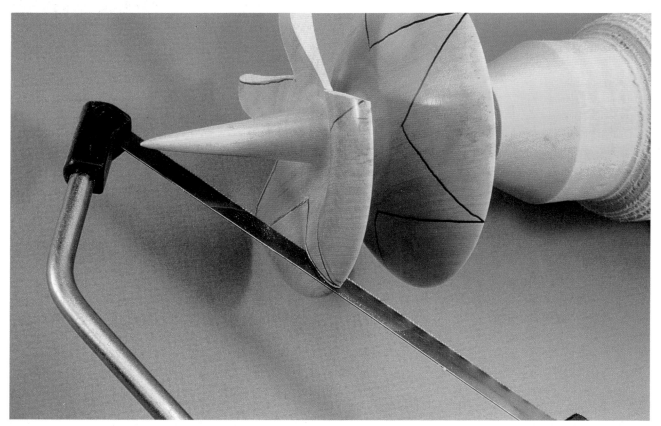

FIG 15.31
Cut along the lines using a mini hacksaw.

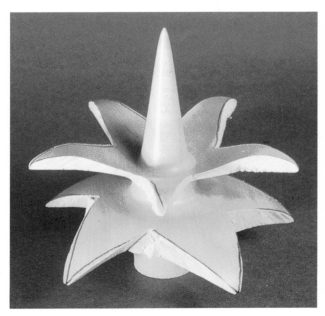

FIG 15.32
The leaf structure, ready to sand and polish.

15 Sand and finish as before, and glue the leaves on to the top of the pineapple.

Fig 15.33 shows the finished box.

FIG 15.33
Two views of the finished 'pineapple' box.

Appendix
Health and Safety in the Workshop

Throughout this book, specific safety precautions have been described in relation to certain procedures and equipment, and readers are advised to refer to these as appropriate. However, some general principles of health and safety should be observed at all times in the workshop.

Machinery

When using machinery, especially items that are designed for cutting, great care should be taken at all times. All blades should be guarded, and fingers and clothing kept well away from moving blades. Always observe the manufacturer's instructions regarding operation, safety, maintenance and storage. Try to avoid operating machinery when you are tired or distracted, as this is when accidents are most likely to occur.

Face Protection

When using a lathe or any other equipment where there is the possibility (however remote) of fragments of wood or other material flying free, facial protection is advisable. There are a variety of safety helmets available, all with face shields, some of which also incorporate respirators. Turners would be well advised to select from the range available to suit their individual needs.

Respiratory Protection

Respiratory problems (both long and short term) caused by the inhalation of fine wood dust seem to be on the increase. Exposing yourself to the risks of temporary or permanent respiratory damage is both foolhardy and unnecessary when there is such a wide range of products available that offer protection.

Disposable masks which cover the nose and mouth are the very minimum form of protection which should be worn. Half-mask respirators are another alternative. Powered respirators, in the form of sealed helmets which provide a flow of clean air over the face, come in various designs.

Ideally, some form of dust extraction system should also be installed in the workshop.

You will need to consider factors such as comfort, degree of exposure to fine dust and the full of range of products available, when deciding upon the method of protection that will best suit your circumstances.

Allergies

Occasionally turners may find that they are allergic to certain timbers. This may be manifested in the form of skin rashes or irritation in the nose and throat. In these instances, it is advisable to avoid exposure to these specific timbers.

Workshop Layout

Many people who do woodturning as a hobby find that they have to work in somewhat cramped conditions. Garden sheds, garages and other small outbuildings are usually the only possible accommodation for a turner who wishes to pursue his or her interest at home. In such circumstances there is usually little choice in the layout of equipment. However, care should still be taken to minimize accidents by storing tools neatly yet accessibly. For example, it should not be necessary to lean across pieces of machinery to gain regular access to turning tools. Tools should be returned to their racks after use, and shavings and other debris swept up. Trailing power cables should be removed and secured carefully.

Similarly, adequate lighting and ventilation in the workshop is essential for safety and comfort.

Common Sense

Much of the above may seem to be common sense, and for most turners, perhaps, these precautions are taken as a matter of course. Having said that, there are occasionally times when we are tired or distracted, or having to work in a hurry and it is then that short cuts are often taken and accidents happen. Most accidents in the workshop can easily be avoided.

BIBLIOGRAPHY

Anderson, T. 'The Ringmaster', *Woodturning*, issue 27, November 1994.

Barton, W. *Chip Carving Patterns*, Sterling, 1990.

Bew, D. 'Stickwork for Use in Woodturning', *Woodturning*, issues 6&7, Jan/Feb & March/April 1992.

Clarke, A. 'Bowl Etching? Blast it!', *Woodturning*, issue 13, March/April 1993.

Cox, J. *Beyond Basic Woodturning*, Stobart, 1993.

Dean, J. *The Craft of Natural Dyeing*, Search Press, 1994.

Hunnex, J. *Woodturning: A Sourcebook of Shapes*, GMC Publications, 1993.

MacTaggart, P. and A. *Practical Gilding*, Mac & Me Ltd, 1985.

Poole, S. *The Complete Pyrography*, GMC Publications, 1995.

Pye, C. *Carving on Turning*, GMC Publications, 1995.

Sanders, J. Colouring Wood, (video), Liberon.

Saylan, M. 'Ebonizing and Bleaching in Black and White', *Woodturning*, issues 7&8, March/April & May/June 1992.

Thurston, V. *The Use of Vegetable Dyes*, Reeves-Dryad Press, 1977.

ABOUT THE AUTHOR

Hilary Bowen was born in Dorchester. She moved to Southampton in 1973 to study psychology at the university, before embarking on a career in teaching. After obtaining an MA in education in 1985, she took up her current post as an education lecturer in a Southampton college of higher education.

Hilary has been woodturning for a number of years now and is the author of *Woodturning Jewellery* (also available from GMC Publications).

She is a member of both the Hampshire Woodturners' Association and the Association of Woodturners of Great Britain. Her work has been on regular display at the Northguild Art Gallery, Southampton. She has also been involved in jewellery making, which has led to her interest in combining wood and metal. It is her intention to explore the possibilities of combining wood with other materials to produce decorative effects on woodturned objects.

METRIC CONVERSION TABLE

INCHES TO MILLIMETRES AND CENTIMETRES						
mm = millimetres cm = centimetres						
inches	mm	cm	inches	cm	inches	cm
⅛	3	0.3	9	22.9	30	76.2
¼	6	0.6	10	25.4	31	78.7
⅜	10	1.0	11	27.9	32	81.3
½	13	1.3	12	30.5	33	83.8
⅝	16	1.6	13	33.0	34	86.4
¾	19	1.9	14	35.6	35	88.9
⅞	22	2.2	15	38.1	36	91.4
1	25	2.5	16	40.6	37	94.0
1¼	32	3.2	17	43.2	38	96.5
1½	38	3.8	18	45.7	39	99.1
1¾	44	4.4	19	48.3	40	101.6
2	51	5.1	20	50.8	41	104.1
2½	64	6.4	21	53.3	42	106.7
3	76	7.6	22	55.9	43	109.2
3½	89	8.9	23	58.4	44	111.8
4	102	10.2	24	61.0	45	114.3
4½	114	11.4	25	63.5	46	116.8
5	127	12.7	26	66.0	47	119.4
6	152	15.2	27	68.6	48	121.9
7	178	17.8	28	71.1	49	124.5
8	203	20.3	29	73.7	50	127.0

INDEX

UPHOLSTERY AND FURNITURE

Care & Repair	*GMC Publications*	Making Shaker Furniture	*Barry Jackson*
Complete Woodfinishing	*Ian Hosker*	Seat Weaving (Practical Crafts)	*Ricky Holdstock*
Furniture Projects	*Rod Wales*	Upholsterer's Pocket Reference Book	*David James*
Furniture Restoration (Practical Crafts)	*Kevin Jan Bonner*	Upholstery: A Complete Course	*David James*
Furniture Restoration & Repair for Beginners	*Kevin Jan Bonner*	Upholstery: Techniques & Projects	*David James*
Green Woodwork	*Mike Abbott*	Woodfinishing Handbook (Practical Crafts)	*Ian Hosker*
Making Fine Furniture	*Tom Darby*		

DOLLS' HOUSES & DOLLS' HOUSE FURNITURE

Architecture for Dolls' Houses	*Joyce Percival*	Making Period Dolls' House Accessories	*Andrea Barham*
The Complete Dolls' House Book	*Jean Nisbett*	Making Period Dolls' House Furniture	*Derek & Sheila Rowbottom*
Easy-to-Make Dolls' House Accessories	*Andrea Barham*	Making Tudor Dolls' Houses	*Derek Rowbottom*
Make Your Own Dolls' House Furniture	*Maurice Harper*	Making Victorian Dolls' House Furniture	*Patricia King*
Making Dolls' House Furniture	*Patricia King*	Miniature Needlepoint Carpets	*Janet Granger*
Making Georgian Dolls' Houses	*Derek Rowbottom*	The Secrets of the Dolls' House Makers	*Jean Nisbett*

OTHER BOOKS

Guide to Marketing	*GMC Publications*	Woodworkers' Career & Educational Source Book	*GMC Publications*

VIDEOS

Carving a Figure: The Female Form	*Ray Gonzalez*	Elliptical Turning	*David Springett*
The Traditional Upholstery Workshop		Woodturning Wizardry	*David Springett*
Part 1: *Drop-in & Pinstuffed Seats*	*David James*	Turning Between Centres: The Basics	*Dennis White*
The Traditional Upholstery Workshop		Turning Bowls	*Dennis White*
Part 2: *Stuffover Upholstery*	*David James*	Boxes, Goblets & Screw Threads	*Dennis White*
Hollow Turning	*John Jordan*	Novelties & Projects	*Dennis White*
Bowl Turning	*John Jordan*	Classic Profiles	*Dennis White*
Sharpening Turning & Carving Tools	*Jim Kingshott*	Twists & Advanced Turning	*Dennis White*
Sharpening the Professional Way	*Jim Kingshott*		

MAGAZINES

WOODTURNING • WOODCARVING • BUSINESSMATTERS

The above represents a full list of all titles currently published or scheduled to be published. All are available direct from the Publishers or through bookshops, newsagents and specialist retailers. To place an order, or to obtain a complete catalogue, contact:

GMC Publications, 166 High Street, Lewes, East Sussex BN7 1XU United Kingdom
Tel: 01273 488005 Fax: 01273 478606

Orders by credit card are accepted

TITLES AVAILABLE FROM
GMC PUBLICATIONS

BOOKS

WOODTURNING

Adventures in Woodturning	David Springett
Bert Marsh: Woodturner	Bert Marsh
Bill Jones' Notes from the Turning Shop	Bill Jones
Carving on Turning	Chris Pye
Colouring Techniques for Woodturners	Jan Sanders
Decorative Techniques for Woodturners	Hilary Bowen
Faceplate Turning: Features, Projects, Practice	GMC Publications
Green Woodwork	Mike Abbott
Illustrated Woodturning Techniques	John Hunnex
Keith Rowley's Woodturning Projects	Keith Rowley
Make Money from Woodturning	Ann & Bob Phillips
Multi-Centre Woodturning	Ray Hopper
Pleasure & Profit from Woodturning	Reg Sherwin
Practical Tips for Turners & Carvers	GMC Publications
Practical Tips for Woodturners	GMC Publications
Spindle Turning	GMC Publications
Turning Miniatures in Wood	John Sainsbury
Turning Wooden Toys	Terry Lawrence
Useful Woodturning Projects	GMC Publications
Woodturning: A Foundation Course	Keith Rowley
Woodturning Jewellery	Hilary Bowen
Woodturning Masterclass	Tony Boase
Woodturning: A Source Book of Shapes	John Hunnex
Woodturning Techniques	GMC Publications
Woodturning Wizardry	David Springett

WOODCARVING

The Art of the Woodcarver	GMC Publications
Carving Birds & Beasts	GMC Publications
Carving Realistic Birds	David Tippey
Carving on Turning	Chris Pye
Decorative Woodcarving	Jeremy Williams
Practical Tips for Turners & Carvers	GMC Publications
Wildfowl Carving Volume 1	Jim Pearce
Wildfowl Carving Volume 2	Jim Pearce
Woodcarving: A Complete Course	Ron Butterfield
Woodcarving for Beginners: Projects, Techniques & Tools	GMC Publications
Woodcarving Tools, Materials & Equipment	Chris Pye

PLANS, PROJECTS, TOOLS & THE WORKSHOP

40 More Woodworking Plans & Projects	GMC Publications
Electric Woodwork: Power Tool Woodworking	Jeremy Broun
The Incredible Router	Jeremy Broun
Making & Modifying Woodworking Tools	Jim Kingshott
Sharpening: The Complete Guide	Jim Kingshott
Sharpening Pocket Reference Book	Jim Kingshott
Woodworking Plans & Projects	GMC Publications
The Workshop	Jim Kingshott

TOYS & MINIATURES

Designing & Making Wooden Toys	Terry Kelly
Heraldic Miniature Knights	Peter Greenhill
Making Board, Peg & Dice Games	Jeff & Jennie Loader
Making Little Boxes from Wood	John Bennett
Making Unusual Miniatures	Graham Spalding
Making Wooden Toys & Games	Jeff & Jennie Loader
Miniature Needlepoint Carpets	Janet Granger
Restoring Rocking Horses	Clive Green & Anthony Dew
Turning Miniatures in Wood	John Sainsbury
Turning Wooden Toys	Terry Lawrence

CREATIVE CRAFTS

The Complete Pyrography	Stephen Poole
Cross Stitch on Colour	Sheena Rogers
Embroidery Tips & Hints	Harold Hayes
Creating Knitware Designs	Pat Ashforth & Steve Plummer
Making Knitware Fit	Pat Ashforth & Steve Plummer
Miniature Needlepoint Carpets	Janet Granger
Tatting Collage: Adventurous Ideas for Tatters	Lindsay Rogers